NATIONAL PUBLIC RADIO

The Cast of Characters

NATIONAL PUBLIC RADIO

The Cast of Characters

by MARY COLLINS

with photographs by

JEROME LIEBLING

and MURRAY BOGNOVITZ

Seven Locks Press

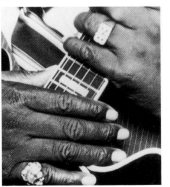

Library of Congress Cataloging-in-Publication Data

Collins, Mary, 1961–
    National Public Radio : the cast of characters / by Mary Collins; with photographs by Jerome Liebling and Murray Bognovitz.
        p.   cm.
    ISBN 0–929765–19–2
    1. National Public Radio—History. 2. Public radio—United States—History. 3. Radio broadcasters—United States—History.
    I. Title.
    HE8697.95.U6C64 1993
    384.54'06'573—dc20   92-34825
                                                              CIP

Manufactured in the United States of America

Book design by Maria Josephy Schoolman
Seven Locks Staff: Kathleen Florio, Lisa Rubarth, Sarah Seage, Norman Sherman

Photo credits appear on pp. 149–150.

SEVEN LOCKS PRESS   WASHINGTON, D.C.   (800) 354–5348

We dedicate this book to all the people, from the beginning, who have made NPR what it is. Many more of them deserved to be mentioned or pictured here, but space and available photographs limited us in telling the whole story. That should not diminish the recognition we intend for the extraordinary and vital job they have done.

Each of us approached this book with deep affection for National Public Radio and its special quality of broadcast journalism. We think it is unique, irreplaceable, and a renewable national resource.

MARY COLLINS

JEROME LIEBLING

MURRAY BOGNOVITZ

Contents

Acknowledgments

Special thanks to all NPR staffers—past and present—who gave so generously of their time, especially Bill Siemering, Charles Bailey, Carolyn Sachs, Jaclin Gilbert and her coworkers in the program library, Bob Edwards and the "Morning Edition" crew. I would also like to acknowledge Kasey Vannett, who provided research assistance on cultural programming, and the editors at Seven Locks Press. On a more personal note, I would like to thank my family, Vivian Spathopoulos, and Jack Hamilton for their encouragement.

—M.C.

Over nine million people listen to NPR newscasts each week. For them, even the headlines, delivered from a tiny sound booth by Carl Kassell (above) and other newscasters, sound better on NPR.

CHAPTER ONE

Backstage

"I'm Bob Edwards. Today is Friday, June 19th, and this is 'Morning Edition.' "

Millions of drowsy Americans wake up every weekday to Edwards's steady, deep Kentucky voice looking for news, the time, and a peculiar sense of security. It's early morning silent, and the host's encouraging tone helps fill the void.

Edwards himself is actually chewing gum and reading a newspaper when National Public Radio fans hear the prerecorded introduction. He sits in the cocoonlike quiet of the gray, compact news studio. Four large microphones fill the table. An old globe lies on a pile of cheap plastic chairs in the corner. The rug smells of mildew.

When Edwards looks up he can see through a large window into the control room, where director Barry Gordemer performs as "part musician, part air-traffic controller." Gordemer makes sure Edwards and Carl Kasell, who delivers the short news updates for the news service, get on and off the air when they're supposed to. It's an exercise that requires exquisite split-second timing.

Gordemer's hand goes up. Edwards leans into the mike. By the time the director drops his hand and the host finishes saying, "It's twenty minutes before the hour," it's *exactly* twenty minutes before the hour. The member stations that carry "Morning Edition" must know precisely when the program cuts from Kasell to Edwards or to a music break; otherwise they're faced with the ultimate nightmare for a sound medium—silence. "A second can be an eternity in broadcasting," says Gordemer.

NPR and the member stations rely on the U.S. Naval Observatory Master Clock, which synchronizes their timers via satellite. At the end of every year the observatory must account for a lost second, so all of the stations' clocks leap forward simultaneously. Gordemer uses a special calculator that adds *time* to help him hit the eight station breaks during the two-hour broadcast. Sometimes Edwards helps fill in a second or two by slowing down his delivery or adding a word that's not in the copy.

It's a tightwire act, which perhaps explains why NPR is so unstructured outside the control room. Edwards lopes across the newsroom in jeans and a casual shirt. Technicians wear shorts. Birkenstock sandals are about as fashionable as the dress code gets, particularly for the overnight crew.

The director can let a bit of the network's quirky side seep into the broadcast with the signature pieces of music played between news items. The staff call the short takes between stories "buttons" and the longer ones used for local station breaks "zippers." Gordemer, who makes the selections for "Morning Edition," describes the process as his "greatest agony and greatest pleasure." He tries to take into account a reporter's style, the tone of the story, and, of course, the time available.

Today he shows up in the control room at 5:30 a.m. with a stack of CDs: the Nuclear Whales Saxophone Orchestra, Makoto Ozone, Mark Sloniker, Eric Marienthal, Ravel piano solo with Abbey Simon.

"Morning Edition" director Barry Gordemer (seen here in tune with some of his best friends) makes the program flow seamlessly from voice to music and back with precise timing and uncanny anticipation and coordination.

Two large racks of music tapes tower over his control panel, one for "Morning Edition" and the other for the ninety-minute evening newsmagazine "All Things Considered." People complained about hearing the same music on both shows, so NPR now has two separate files. The labels on the sides of the tapes describe the mood and length of the music rather than the title or performer. So if Gordemer decides at the last minute he doesn't want the Nuclear Whales sax piece, he can scan the labels and make a quick switch. "Sad, mopey flute II," "One jiggly note," "Tense notes," and "Nice guitar and orchestra" are just some of the options.

Occasionally a director has a particular song in mind. During the Oliver North hearings, for example, someone decided that a generic piece like "Mopey flute" just wouldn't do; so they selected an instrumental piece titled "We Don't Need Another Hero." And some brave soul at "All Things Considered" decided to play the jazz piece "An Incredibly Troubled Brother" after a story on the many problems of Marion Barry, then mayor of Washington, D.C.

"These are very subtle jokes," laughs one technician.

"They can get you into trouble," says Gordemer, with a smile. "Most people will never know, but it *is* editorializing with music."

This morning there are no tricks and no switches. A report from special correspondent Cokie Roberts is on the air. "She sounds awful," says Gordemer. "She's losing her voice."

Edwards talks into the intercom. "What's wrong with Cokie? This is worse than election night when she did ABC and us."

Later he comments on how distracting that can be for a listener—especially NPR fans, who seem to take an unusually personal interest in the network's stars. "They aren't listening to what she's saying. They're thinking, 'Oh my God, Cokie's hurting.'"

Roberts's overworked voice fades away as Edwards prepares to shift into the longest uninterrupted segment of the show. "Rebuilding south central Los

Angeles could be delayed . . ." His head shakes as he carefully stresses certain syllables. His tone is noticeably brighter and livelier than his off-the-air conversational voice.

While Edwards continues the broadcast, the technicians start talking about the "chair video."

The office equipment at NPR is at best drab, at worst just plain unusable. At one point the shortage of functional chairs reached crisis proportions. Carl Kasell claims it got so bad he had to tie his chair down to keep others from stealing it.

When no aid floated down from management, several people decided to videotape staffers in their various states of broken-chair misery. The tape wound up on the desk of NPR President Doug Bennet. "It did the trick," says Gordemer, who now has several very nice, high, blue-cushioned chairs behind his control desk.

The chatter suddenly stops. Kasell is on the air, and two members of Congress have just joined Edwards in the studio for a live discussion on the urban aid bill. When Gordemer switches back to Edwards, a technician begins pushing small levers on a cluttered control panel, making subtle adjustments for tone and loudness to even out the voices of the three speakers. She's having trouble with the voice of the representative from Connecticut. "She sounds like she's in a tunnel," one technician says nervously.

Gordemer complains that Edwards is mumbling. They amplify his voice and try to deepen the congresswoman's. Gordemer cautions the person at the controls. "Remember to change the level on Edwards's voice when he comes back with the regular broadcast; otherwise he'll sound like he's booming."

NPR listeners identify with the people they hear. When Cokie Roberts occasionally gets hoarse, they vicariously suffer and express concern. In good voice or bad, she often broadcasts from the comfort of the home where she has lived since she was a child.

The director's speaker phone rings suddenly, and a voice says, "The tone on left is from Tallahassee." It's Red Barber.

"Hello, Red. How are you?" Gordemer says. "You're in good voice this morning."

The representatives leave the studio. Jean Cochran does a short newscast from Carl Kasell's booth, while Edwards prepares for his weekly conversation with Red. A button plays. Gordemer signals Edwards, who provides a brief lead-in, then says, "Hello, Red."

"Good morning, Bob."

They sound like two southerners talking baseball on their front porch. They both get excited about the fact that Edwards is going to throw out the game ball at this week's Detroit Tigers–Boston Red Sox game.

3

The technicians just sit back and watch Edwards operate. They close the show with a prerecorded review of the movie "Batman Returns" by *Washington Post* critic Tom Shales. Shales calls the sequel "a bigger, infinitely noisier bore" than the original Batman movie.

Edwards takes off his glasses, puts them in his shirt, and turns off the lamp. It's exactly 7:59 a.m.

The executive producer for morning news, Bob Ferrante, bounds around the newsroom in a jet-set, light green suit and pink tie. He looks like he just got back from Florida. The day shift has arrived. Some of the night-owl staffers leave, but key players like Edwards and Gordemer must stay until noon just in case there's a breaking story or a section of the show taped earlier needs revision.

Ferrante and his staff normally begin preparing for the 8:45 a.m. story meeting, which sets the agenda for the next day's broadcast; but today is Friday, the end of the workweek for the "Morning Edition" crew. The night staff gets a few days off. "Those people suffer enough," says senior editor Vicki O'Hara. "The first four or five years I was here I worked those hours [2 a.m. to noon]. . . . You never adjust. You're always tired. You're depressed because you're out of sync with the world around you. You don't see your friends. You don't see your family. . . . It's not good to do it for too long."

People rarely last more than a year or two on the night shift, which makes Edwards's stay of thirteen years all the more remarkable. "But that's what radio is—dependable old Bob," he says. "You're groggy in the morning. You want to know that everything's okay with the world. The coffee still smells the same. Bob is there."

Of course, Bob is there only if things go well in Record Central (RC), Production Master Control (PMC), and the satellite distribution center known as MOTC, short for Main Origination Technical Center.

Reporters call in stories from all over the world on telephone lines not always suited to the sound quality necessary for good radio. Technicians in RC and PMC try to work out the static and background noise on everything they tape and then time the segments to the second so directors and producers can have some idea what they're working with. When things get really frantic, as they did during the Gulf War, technicians sometimes have to hand over the actual reel of tape instead of the nicely packaged and spruced-up cartridges they call "carts." Edwards says that at several points during the war they just put the reel in the tape machine in the control room and let it unwind onto the floor. There wasn't even enough time to hook it up to the rewind wheel.

A second can be an eternity in broadcasting. —Barry Gordemer, director of "Morning Edition"

The RC sits off to the side of the newsroom, while the PMC, which tends to handle less time-factored material, takes up space one floor down. Its huge control panels and row of tape machines make it look like some kind of supercomputer from the 1950s.

Down the hall from the PMC, a Washington, D.C., license plate hanging next to the door of the satellite center reads: NPR-MOTC. In many ways that room does drive the network.

Ralph Woods, manager of satellite operations, tunes in to a local radio station that is airing a Celtic music program, "Thistle and Shamrock," currently being carried on the satellite. "See those reels turning very slowly over there?" He points into a large room that looks like control central for NASA. In the far right-hand corner two reels rotate methodically. "Well, the distance from those reels to this speaker"—he jabs his thumb toward the radio on his desk—"is 46,000 miles," the distance to the satellite and back.

Two TV-size screens over Woods's head carry a list of programs scheduled to be broadcast via satellite that day: "Thistle and Shamrock," "Talk of the Nation," "Fresh Air," and non-NPR programs like "Monitor Radio." Although the network is MOTC's primary customer, it does not own or operate the satellite system. Congress decided it wouldn't be a good idea to have the primary program producer for public radio also be in charge of program distribution. So NPR buys space along with the Christian Science Monitor, American Public Radio, and others.

There's a five-digit number next to each program on the screen. That's the precise time the satellite will switch away. So if "Talk of the Nation" host John Hockenberry isn't ready to sign off his call-in show at exactly 3:59.10 . . . ZAP. He's cut off anyway.

Woods and his crew seem even more offbeat than the "Morning Edition" night staff. On a wall near his desk Woods has what looks like a map of the stars; but the points of light are satellites, a man-made galaxy of hundreds of orbiting transponders. The technicians call the huge machine in the main room

When Bob Edwards gets to the studio each weekday morning around 2:30 a.m., only a few colleagues are already at work. Most of the nation is still sound asleep as Edwards faces another day of interviews and stories that inform and delight.

7

Bullwinkle, "because it's such a moose," he says. Most of the workers in MOTC are men who look as though they hid in their garages when they were kids and tinkered with homemade radio transmitters. They show the joy of having an avocation become a vocation.

"You should have seen what we went through to get Salman Rushdie on the air," says Woods, referring to the author whose controversial book, *The Satanic Verses,* led the Iranian government to call for his assassination. "He wouldn't come here—not that we wanted him." The staffers laugh. The author wanted to push the paperback release of *The Satanic Verses* on John Hockenberry's "Talk of the Nation." The MOTC crew decided to air Rushdie from an undisclosed location in the Washington area.

Technicians from PMC and MOTC piled in a van with a mobile uplink and headed for Dulles Airport, where they were supposed to meet "Mr. Bell." He wasn't there. Instead they were told to follow a nondescript gray sedan, which took a circuitous route to a distant hotel. "Mr. Bell" was somewhere inside. The rain came down in streams as they set up their equipment. With just ninety seconds to spare, they finally got a clear audio signal to the MOTC control center

back at NPR. "That was a close one," says Mike Starling, director of PMC.

After a brief pause in the conversation, another technician starts talking enthusiastically about the ultimate satellite horror show: sun transit. Twice a year, during the spring and fall equinoxes, the sun lines up with the satellite and the earth. Such a direct hit of solar energy overloads the satellite receivers; for about five minutes there's nothing but static. The blank band arrives at a different time for each station as the satellite and earth rotate around the sun. "So we send each station a message. Something like, 'From 13:28 to 13:33 your signal will be toast,'" says Woods.

Starling laughs. Later, while walking back to his office, he confides that he ground his own glass lenses when he was a boy and just loved astronomy.

It's 2:30 p.m., which is crunch time for the PMC staff. They need to get in material, or "feeds," for "All Things Considered," which airs at 5:00.

NPR has about seventy-five people who specialize in "moving electrons," says Starling, which is more than any other radio network, including Voice of America. The huge investment in high-quality sound has earned NPR a reputation for producing "movies for the ear."

"We really do believe that the audience will notice the technical quality; that these pieces are alive and vibrant, that they take you to the scene," he says. "It takes a lot of care and time in production to do."

One floor above Starling, the "All Things Considered" staff also heads toward its zero hour. Unlike the morning news program, which has people working nearly round-the-clock, "ATC" basically starts with a blank slate every day. The editors, producers, and hosts begin with a 10:00 a.m. story meeting, which melts into a joint meeting at 10:30 with the news staff from both of NPR's daily news programs. People read the paper, shuffle in and out. At one point someone passes out a ten-page list of possible or assigned stories for the day. Noah Adams sits in shorts and a long-sleeved T-shirt reading the paper. Occasionally he joins an ongoing discussion. The conference table is oblong, but somehow "ATC" host Robert Siegel, with his beard and professorial voice, is clearly the center.

By 3:00 several of the topics discussed in the morning meeting have made it onto the large white storyboard in the center of the "ATC" newsroom. It's a remarkably steady day. Sometimes the entire lineup can shift less than an hour before airtime. This time everything seems set by 3:35.

In Edit Booth Four, assistant producer Akili Tyson works on the taped phone interview that Robert Siegel had earlier in the day with South African author Rian Malan. Malan is disgusted by the claim of the African National Congress (ANC) that President F. W. de Klerk's government had something to do with the deaths of forty people hacked to pieces by a band of men from the Inkatha Freedom party.

Tyson has cut and pasted all day as he tries to trim the piece to three-and-a-half minutes. Whole sections of the conversation replay again and again in the newsroom as he tries to decide exactly where to slice. Several times he lets out a muted scream and leaves the tape room.

By 3:35 he must pick up the pace. He runs the tape so fast that Siegel and Malan sound like cartoon chipmunks. By 4:35 every tape machine in the newsroom is on chipmunk mode. Indeed, even though the ninety-minute newsmagazine has a much more luxurious pace on the air than "Morning Edition," behind the scenes the staff is markedly more tense than their morning counterparts. They must complete each story from beginning to end by 4:30 each day. There is no "overnight" desk.

The only lull in the afternoon comes from a far corner of the room where a young woman practices a violin piece behind a gray partition next to Siegel's office. Her bow rises and falls above the wall as the clear notes sing out over the clatter of the newsroom and the tape machine. She captures the pace and tender tone of the show itself even though, ironically, she has no part in it. She's working on something for another producer.

Executive producer Ellen Weiss more accurately reflects the backstage frenzy. She can't find her drink. Her phone rings. She just unplugs it.

By 4:45 Weiss and Noah Adams are arguing in the control room over the

The morning meeting—a moment of chaotic repose —begins the day's preparation for "All Things Considered" with a search for stories by both on- and off-air talent. Robert Siegel (right) —reporter, host, and administrator— has played all those roles in the morning meetings.

length of some piece. Tapecutters run. Phones slam. The *Chicago Tribune*, *The New York Times*, *The Christian Science Monitor*, and other newspapers lie scattered across the tables. Former "ATC" host Susan Stamberg floats through, decked out in a brilliant turquoise jacket and black skirt. She chats briefly with Robert Siegel, who has left the studio to get a glass of water. The slogan on his mug reads, "Symphony of Sound."

Once "All Things Considered" is on the air, director Bob Boilen must orchestrate two hosts and newscaster Corey Flintoff. There is little banter among the technicians in the control booth as Boilen moves through the show.

Siegel's piece on Malan airs at the top of the final half hour. "Whoa, this is getting pretty gloomy," notes Boilen. He reaches behind him for a lighter button. Less than a minute before the original music is supposed to air, he makes the switch.

Adams clicks away at a computer next to his microphone whenever he and Siegel are not on the air. They sit at opposite ends of the table.

Adams's gentle voice follows the movie reviews. "The executive producer is Ellen Weiss. I'm Noah Adams." Then his cohost closes: "And I'm Robert Siegel. It's 'All Things Considered.'"

"The news is next" introduces newscasters like Corey Flintoff (above) and focuses listener attention on the day's headlines. Newscasts were once rejected by stations as modeled too much on a commercial pattern, but they now add a desirable element to NPR news coverage.

CHAPTER TWO

The Family Tree

Now that NPR has become a habit for millions of Americans, it's easy to forget that programs like "Morning Edition" and "All Things Considered" haven't always been around. Their gestation took decades.

First land-grant universities, like the University of Wisconsin, had to pioneer their distinctive blend of educational programming, which went beyond classroom lectures and piano music to social commentary and community affairs. Then Edward R. Murrow had to set the standard for serious radio news with his World War II broadcasts from London. Finally Congress had to figure out how to create a public broadcasting network that required government funding but kept government fingers out of the programming pie. The Public Broadcasting Act of 1967 did everything but that, which left the door open for many of the problems that have plagued public broadcasting from the 1970s to the present.

Actually Congress did make the key decision not to give the government control over content on the airwaves in 1918. The navy had monopolized radio during World War I for its ship-to-shore communications. After the war the navy wanted to maintain its hold on the medium, but an indignant Congress turned it down. "Having just won a fight against autocracy, we would start an autocratic movement with this bill," exclaimed one House member.

At the time fewer than 60,000 Americans owned radio sets, but the government's hands-off policy opened the floodgates. By 1928, approximately 7.5 million households had a radio. By the 1930s it had clearly arrived as a mass medium.

Listeners often heard more than an ear could stand. The lack of government regulation meant that anybody could launch a radio program. The airwaves became cluttered with overlapping signals. A woman spreading the gospel from her basement in California could have just as strong a signal as a full-fledged variety show outside New York. And the man in charge of the cleanup, Secretary of Commerce Herbert Hoover, lacked the statutory authority to do anything about it. When he tried to realign the system, the stations dragged him into court, where he lost. Congress bailed the secretary out in 1927 by passing the Dill-White Radio Act, which gave the government discretion over licensing and created the Federal Radio Commission (later the Federal Communications Commission, or FCC). In an important tip of the hat to the stations, the bill also explicitly prohibited government intrusion into programming.

That same year NBC became the first national radio network and began distributing programming to small commercial stations starved for something to put on the air. Most of them operated on a shoestring budget that forced them to rely on second-rate local sopranos and long periods of silent downtime. Now, for a small fee, they could broadcast an opera out of New York or a comedy routine out of Chicago. A year later William Paley, son of a New York cigar manufacturer, launched CBS.

The astounding success of some commercial programming, like "Amos 'n' Andy," which reached 40 million listeners in 1929-30, proved that radio could be a lucrative mass medium that attracted national sponsors. Investors began seeing dollar signs on the radio spectrum and flooded the FCC in the mid-1930s with license applications. The effects on noncommercial radio were immediate, and not always good. To make way for the booming commercial market, the small-town, low-budget community and college stations that had sprung up in the unregulated 1920s were pressured to change. Instead, with virtually no cash reserves, those stations closed down or sold out at an alarming rate. By 1938, 164 of the 202 licensed educational stations had gone off the air.

Broadcasting was an agrarian term. It means the scattering of seeds. If you look in a dictionary from 1901, that's the only definition you'll find. —Bill Siemering, NPR's first program director

The National Association of Educational Broadcasters (NAEB), which could surely be called the grandfather of public radio, started pressuring the FCC to allocate a specific number of channels just for educational programming. By 1945 the NAEB got what it wanted—twenty FM channels from 88 to 92 megahertz. Educational stations now had a claim on the low end of the radio dial. The only question was, how would they fill the space?

Land-grant schools like the University of Wisconsin had already found an answer. Indeed, the quality programming at Wisconsin's WHA and similar state university stations had a lot to do with why the FCC handed over the channels to begin with. Bill Siemering, NPR's first program director, remembers listening to WHA as a boy growing up in Madison, Wisconsin, in the 1940s. "When I was a kid I went to a two-room country school; and twice a day we would tune in to the radio, and I would learn about science, art, music, and social studies—all from the radio. They even had a teacher's manual.

"It was broadcast by the University of Wisconsin, which is where public broadcasting began in this country. It was one of these large land-grant universities, and the motto was that the boundaries of the campus were the boundaries of the state. So radio was ideally suited for that."

Land-grant universities in Ohio, Michigan, Illinois, and other midwestern states created similar networks. These stations brought music to farmers in their fields and live radio dramas to children sitting at home. They offered lectures on agriculture and philosophy, on homemaking and carpentry. They brought society to the hinterlands.

"'Broadcasting' was an agrarian term," Siemering points out. "It means

14

the scattering of seeds. If you look in a dictionary from 1901, that's the only definition you'll find.

"There was an almost romantic appeal to using radio to scatter seeds of knowledge and culture to the rural population of the Midwest. Most of the farm homes had a piano and a radio. After they got portables, they could listen on the tractor."

While the state universities were pioneering their vision of public service cultural programming in the 1940s, Edward R. Murrow was leaving his indelible mark on radio news. The commercial networks, particularly NBC, put

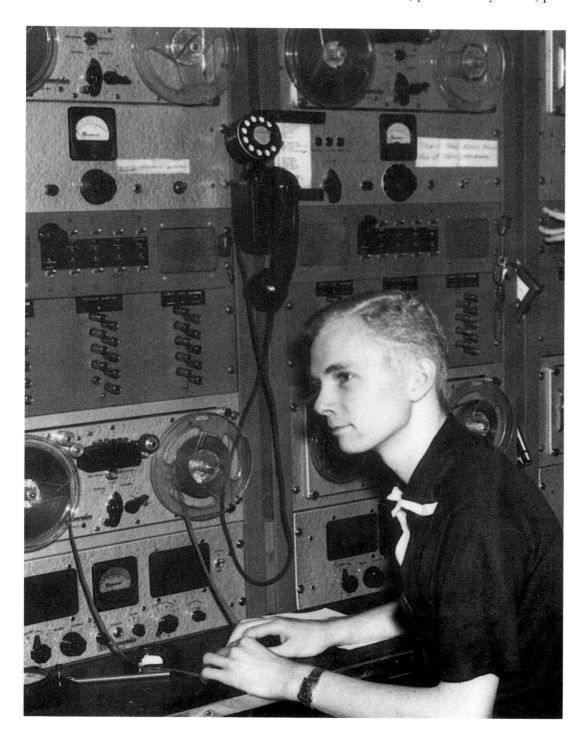

No one has been more vital to the evolution of public radio than Bill Siemering, shown here during his college days at WHA in Madison, Wisconsin. NPR board member, station manager, creator of programs, and counselor to newcomers to radio, Siemering has combined vision, wisdom, and a gentle nature as an important and continuing influence.

15

most of their dollars into entertainment because it drew larger audiences and advertisers. Murrow's World War II broadcasts helped show that radio could be a legitimate and popular news medium.

Before the war most stations would just have an announcer read from the local paper for five minutes; many didn't even bother with that. Ed Bliss, former newswriter for Murrow and Walter Cronkite, remembers his first job as a newscaster for a station in Columbus, Ohio, in 1936. It had its own newscast, but "it was still very rudimentary," Bliss says. "It was just a reporter's desk and a lamp. When that lamp winked on, you looked at the clock and you read the script you had written for fifteen minutes according to that clock and then you stopped. There wasn't any director."

He'd come in at 1 a.m. to prepare copy for the 7:30 a.m. broadcast. "All the time I worked there, I never met a single person."

This limited foray into radio news was enough to earn him a job on the overnight desk at CBS in New York. He eventually worked his way to the day shift for the fifteen-minute news program "Edward R. Murrow with the News."

"Murrow was very careful with his facts," Bliss recalls, "and he wanted the news presented very simply, in a straightforward way. When I came on, a guy told me to keep a packet of Camels in my pocket because Ed would ask for a smoke. 'And don't give him adjectives,' he said."

Murrow's bare-bones style became familiar to millions during World War II as he broadcast the sounds of war and sorrow from the bombed-out streets of London. "The noise that you hear at this moment is the sound of the air-raid siren," he told listeners during an August 1940 broadcast of "London After Dark."

"People are walking along very quietly. We're just at the entrance of an air-raid shelter here, and I must move the cable over just a bit so people can walk in."

A. M. Sperber, author of *Murrow: His Life and Times,* describes the rest of the newscast: "As 30 million Americans listened, [Murrow] let the open microphone pick up the howling sirens, the hollow clang of the shelter door, the anti-aircraft guns in counterpoint to the chugging buses . . . He crouched down on the sidewalk to pick up the sounds of passersby walking unhurriedly to the shelter, their footsteps audible, their bodies invisible in the murk, 'like ghosts shod with steel shoes.'"

"Sound tells the story," says producer Jay Kernis (above). "It all goes back to Edward R. Murrow (opposite page) reporting and saying, 'I am laying the microphone on the ground so you can hear the tanks.'"

Such sound portraits aroused American sympathies and helped precipitate U.S. involvement in the war. "It was not a new technique—prewar broadcasts had caught the sound of bat and ball at cricket matches—but it was a new use of sound, conveying an attitude, a point in history," Sperber writes. "The Murrow broadcasts became a national listening habit."

As professor of broadcast journalism at American University in Washington, D.C., Bliss passed on Murrow's gospel for good radio to his students, which included a whole generation of NPR staffers, like Bob Edwards, David Molpus, Alex Chadwick, Jean Cochran, and Jackie Judd. "Ed was accused of teaching Edward R. Murrow One and Edward R. Murrow Two," says Bob Edwards. "What better way could you teach?

"Murrow's important because he set the standard very early. If someone else had been doing the news in those days—you know all those tabloid programs that we have today—if they had been in the early broadcast programs, then that would have been the way we went."

Jay Kernis, creator and former producer of "Morning Edition," credits Murrow with introducing the idea that pure sound could tell a story: "It all goes back to Edward R. Murrow reporting and saying, 'I am laying the microphone on the ground so you can hear the tanks.' Remember the top award in public radio is the Edward R. Murrow Award."

If Bliss and Murrow mark one branch of the family tree for NPR programming, Bill Siemering surely stands on the other. He not only listened to the University of Wisconsin's WHA, he worked there as a board operator, writer, actor, and newscaster. In 1962 he used his radio experience to get a job as manager of a student station at the State University of New York in Buffalo, WBFO. By the time he left in 1970 to become the first program director for NPR, he had a new, fuller vision of what public radio could be.

"I started [at WBFO] with the Wisconsin model," he says, "but it didn't work in an urban environment. I realized we needed to do something different." So the station set up in a predominantly low-income black neighborhood and did special programs on minority artists. They produced a show called "City Links," which just played the sounds of the city—from people changing shifts at a factory to an airplane flying over Buffalo. They ran "City Links" updates throughout the day like newscasts. When students protested the school's administration in 1970 by rioting, WBFO worked round-the-clock airing material from all sides. "I tried to say that radio is alive, that radio is inclusive," says Siemering. "I tried to use sound to tell stories."

He attracted writers like Robert Creeley and future NPR talent like science correspondent Ira Flatow, former "ATC" host Mike Waters, and former director Rich Firestone. Siemering's unique combination of minority and mainstream cultural programming became the model for Terry Gross's immensely popular cultural show, "Fresh Air," which now has more than a million NPR listeners. He created one of the first truly "public" stations by taking a step beyond the land-grant university radio he had loved as a boy.

The gospel of good radio came from Murrow through Ed Bliss (left), an inspiring teacher of broadcast journalism, and through his students, including (clockwise from left) Bob Edwards, Alex Chadwick, Jean Cochran, and David Molpus.

Public radio flowered in both city and country, serving different audiences in special ways. At WHA, Bill Siemering (center) and others brought drama to a largely rural audience.

While clearly the leader in this kind of community radio work, Siemering was not alone. "There was this small group of us doing this kind of stuff," he says. "It was not just educational radio. It was a bridge. That's what working in an urban environment forced us to do."

As Siemering carved and crafted in Buffalo, another city station—WRVR, run by the Riverside Church in New York City—also shaped shows and trained staffers who would later influence NPR. Former "Morning Edition" producer Jay Kernis started there as an intern when he was sixteen. Robert Siegel served as news director. "WRVR had a newsmagazine program—so to speak," Siegel says with a laugh, "and a two-hour morning news show. . . . Neal Conan passed through. Adam Powell became director of news later on."

"A lot of people who are in the business today worked there. It did a lot of experimental stuff," says Kernis. "It did a lot of shows that became prototypes for NPR shows. That's the reason NPR knew that it needed something like 'All Things Considered.'"

While Siemering, Siegel, Kernis, and others built bridges, Congress grappled with legislation that would eventually create the Corporation for Public Broadcasting. One of the key issues was how to clarify the distinction between *educational* and *public* programming. Until 1967 the terms had been used interchangeably to refer to the instructional-type shows generally aired on noncommercial TV and radio stations. But the work at WBFO, WRVR, WHA, and other unique stations had given new meaning to the word *public*.

As with most issues related to public radio, however, the debate actually began because of concerns over content on public *television*. Educators won the right to a piece of the TV spectrum in the 1940s, but they lacked the resources to do anything with the airtime. Congress helped out a bit in 1962 with the Educational Television Facilities Act, which provided limited money for programming; but public TV fare remained pretty slim and largely instructional.

The picture changed when President Lyndon Johnson decided to add his considerable weight to the cause. He believed a government-funded broadcasting network could make great use of all that noncommercial space and would become a "vital resource to enrich our homes." He turned to the Carnegie Corporation for a blueprint.

Starting in 1965, the Carnegie Commission on Educational Television spent two years and interviewed 225 people before publishing its report, *Public Television: A Program for Action,* which drew a clear line between *educational* and *public.* The network the commission envisioned would be the latter and "would be different from any now in existence. It is not the educational television we now know."

The commission's twelve recommendations touched upon many of the things that Siemering and others were already doing: diversified programming that included minority voices; public affairs programming that explored controversial contemporary issues; artistic programming that tapped into musicians, painters, sculptors, actors, and singers from around the world.

In the report, the commission ran a letter from E. B. White that captures the essence of what was so new about its vision of *public* broadcasting:

> Noncommercial television should address itself to the ideal of excellence, not the idea of acceptability—which is what keeps commercial television from climbing the staircase. I think television should be the visual counterpart of the literary essay, should arouse our dreams, satisfy our hunger for beauty, take us on journeys, enable us to participate in events, present great drama and music, explore the sea and the sky and the woods and the hills. It should be our Lyceum, our Chautauqua, our Minsky's and our Camelot. It should restate and clarify the social dilemma and the political pickle.

In New York City on WNYC, Mayor Fiorello LaGuardia read the "funnies" when newspapers were on strike. Public radio did things other stations would not.

In the commission's words, *public* broadcasting would address "all that is of human interest and importance" not currently supported by advertisers.

President Johnson took up this vision and urged Congress to enact legislation based on the commission's findings—the Public Television Act of 1967.

A few months later Johnson stood before the House insisting that radio be added to the act. This sudden jump was actually a logical leap for the president. He had built his political career on profits from a radio station in Austin, Texas, that he had bought in 1943 for just $17,500. His investment blossomed into a $7-million asset with an average annual net earning of $500,000. So when radio advocates turned to Johnson, they found a very sympathetic ear. His own experience in broadcasting had shown him that radio remained a powerful, popular medium despite the advent of the television age.

In a March speech before Congress on the public television act, he pointedly included radio in every line item: "Increase federal funds for television and radio facility construction. . . . Create a corporation for public television authorized to provide support to noncommercial television and radio. . . . Noncommercial television and radio in America, even though supported by Federal funds, must be absolutely free from any Federal Government interference. . . ."

In *The History of Public Broadcasting*, authors John Witherspoon and Roselle Kovitz claim that "perhaps the most divisive issue of 1967 for public broadcasters was whether to include radio in the act. Opponents argued that the educational radio system's long history of weakness would drag the entire Carnegie effort into oblivion."

In 1967, President Lyndon Johnson insisted that public radio no longer be treated as an unwanted child. He signed into law (above with Sen. John Pastore to his right) a bill "to provide support to non-commercial television and radio."

Critics pointed to the vast number of noncommercial stations that had annual budgets under $10,000. A third of these stations allocated less than a thousand dollars a year for the purchase of programming. To be successfully incorporated into an effective national public network, they would need money, and that concerned the advocates of the fledgling public television industry far more than the issue of quality programming.

Once again the key crusader for public radio came from the National Association of Educational Broadcasters—director Jerrold Sandler. In his testimony before Congress he cited the successes of stations like WBUR in Boston, which had produced five hours of news programming during a local newspaper strike, and WUOT in Knoxville, which offered its rural listeners fifty hours of music recorded from the Library of Congress.

"Make no mistake about it, radio is *not* television without pictures," he said. "Public radio has a whole wealth of services, far more complex . . . and unique than those that television has to offer. 'No medium,' [former CBS President] Fred Friendly has said, 'can match radio for speed and ease of

22

contact on a worldwide basis. One lone man, wandering a continent with a small tape recorder, can send back wonders.'"

Sandler's poetic plea wouldn't have been enough if many of Johnson's "Great Society" Democrats hadn't elected to side with their party leader. Rep. Claude Pepper of Florida, who went on to become one of the longest serving members in the House, was the first to go on record in favor of public radio. The consummate New Dealer in the 1930s, Representative Pepper had no qualms about spending tax dollars for a public service. "I was at Harvard Law School before I ever lived in a city where there was a gallery or where there was an opportunity to hear good music," he said. "Today there is no excuse for the most remotely resident American not to have an opportunity to enjoy the best cultural influences and activities in all the world." And no medium was better suited for this democratic purpose, he claimed, than radio.

Ironically, the American public of the cynical sixties wasn't so sure it wanted a government-funded broadcasting network. People feared it would become a conduit for propaganda and political grandstanding. "I, as well as many of my colleagues in both Houses, have recently been deluged by mail in opposition to this legislation," Representative Pepper said. "Most of this correspondence has called the bill 'Hitler-type propaganda ministry.' Mr. Chairman," he added, "this couldn't be further from the truth."

Throughout the remainder of the hearings, supporters of the bill continually emphasized the public nature of the project and promised protection against government interference. "This system is to be constructed on the firm foundation of a strong and energetic system of local stations," insisted Dr. James R. Killian, who had chaired the Carnegie Commission on Educational Television. "The heart of the system is to be the community."

Johnson's many supporters, who included Killian, eventually silenced the antiradio contingent, but the stickier issues of government meddling and funding became a quagmire. Fred Friendly, a Columbia University journalism professor at the time, felt it necessary to issue a warning, "a warning because birth defects would make such a service too weak and dependent to achieve the high goals" the commission had set out. "Public television is going to need money—lots of it." The politicians in charge of handing over the cash had to be open-minded enough to let the public broadcasting system "rock the boat," Friendly said. "There should be times when every man in politics will wish it had never been created."

"Write it in the report," Sen. John Pastore interjected at that point. "What we should say in the report is that all of us agree that our problem is money, that the more public money you put into this, the more you endanger the freedom of expression."

The tension threatened to kill the bill. The various camps compromised by cutting out all references to funding; prohibiting all forms of editorializing (a ban that wasn't lifted until 1982); and by vaguely promising to set up some kind of corporation that could serve as a protective barrier between the public

Rare men, rare advocates: Congressman Claude Pepper (top) and James R. Killian (above), chair of the Carnegie Commission on Educational Television, were persuasive advocates for an enterprise built on "a firm foundation of a strong and energetic system of local stations."

23

television and radio stations and the government. The loopholes Congress left behind plagued the public broadcasting system for decades.

The battle over money continued into 1968. First the newly formed Corporation for Public Broadcasting (CPB) would get $20 million; then the offer went down to $9 million, and finally $5 million. The Vietnam War had drained the treasury; it was no time for costly start-up programs.

The Carnegie Commission, CBS, and the Communications Workers of America had to ride in on a white horse with millions of dollars to fill the funding gap. The Ford Foundation single-handedly pledged $20 million for public TV and radio.

These generous donations gave CPB the breathing room it needed to get off the ground. But as the Johnson adminstration gave way to the Nixon White House, there was a foreboding sense that the federal government might never find an answer to the long-range funding question. For the time being, public broadcasting would have to rely largely on private handouts.

The following year CPB convened a conference in San Diego for radio station managers, who hammered out a plan for what would eventually become National Public Radio. Unlike its TV counterpart, the Public Broadcasting Service (PBS), NPR was expected to produce—not just distribute—programming.

CPB asked Bill Siemering to help direct the discussion because of a poignant essay, entitled "Public Radio: Some Essential Ingredients," that he had written that year in a trade journal. In it he exclaimed that a national public radio network should be "on the frontier of the contemporary and help create new tastes; public radio should be an aural museum—an available source of musical and literary masterpieces.

"But public broadcasting can no longer be content as a refreshing cultural oasis," he added. "It must also supply the basic nutrients to save the life of the public from information starvation."

The NPR vision had been set. The format had been set. The only thing that remained in question was money.

John Macy, the first president of CPB, told Siemering and other members of CPB's radio advisory committee that "we like radio, but television has a lot of real pressing needs right now. I've got to give my attention to television." Attention translated into funding. Over the next decade NPR received less than 10 percent of the public broadcasting budget. Radio's sideshow status became a given.

The Formative Years

Siemering immediately placed his imprint on the fledgling network by choosing to have the voice of a young black drug addict included in the debut of NPR's newsmagazine "All Things Considered" on May 3, 1971. In dreamy tones the woman explained what it was like to have "Harry [heroin] come knockin' at your door." Her soft speech captured the allure and lunacy of the addiction cycle.

He had laid out his master plan for the news show at the same San Diego conference that gave birth to the network. "It will be more than just a transmission of data or the 'hard' news," he told station managers. "It will transmit the experience of people and institutions from as widely varying backgrounds and areas as are feasible. It will advance the art and enjoyment of the sound medium. Speaking with many voices and dialects, it will be national. It will be the essence of radio."

As NPR's first programming director, Siemering had the job he needed to turn his brainchild into a reality. He looked for talent that "salivated" at the prospect of working on an entirely new kind of broadcasting. Men with navy radio experience would come in with all the technical expertise, but Siemering would turn them down in favor of people who had never put their voice on a radio wave.

He sought out experienced print reporters, like Robert Conley from *The New York Times,* who became the first "ATC" host. He looked to his past for people like former WBFO reporter Mike Waters and to the future by pulling in talented young women such as Linda Wertheimer before women's voices were thought professional enough for broadcast news.

"It had to be journalistically sound. Period. Balanced, accurate, engaging," he says. "Secondly, we wanted to use radio imaginatively, to reach more listeners; to make it accessible so that it didn't sound like we were dressed in a tux or that we were speaking with British accents."

"All Things Considered" managed to meet Siemering's lofty standards on a remarkably consistent basis in the early years, despite the lack of funding and a relatively green staff. The top story on the first broadcast had an immediacy to it that became NPR's trademark. Thousands of antiwar demonstrators had converged on Washington, D.C., in what would be the final mass protest against U.S. involvement in Vietnam. NPR reporter Jeff Kamen cruised the crowds with his tape recorder as the police made more than 7,000 arrests.

"Excuse me, Sergeant," Kamen said. "Is that a technique—where the men actually try to drive the motorcycles right into the demonstrators?"

"Naw, it's no technique," the officer replied. "We're trying to go down the road and the people get in front of you. What are you gonna do? You don't stop on a dime."

The on-the-street interview captured the tension, the chanting, the sounds of youthful anger and government indifference. But such layered pieces took time and careful editing. The work wore on the young staff. How could they possibly put out a ninety-minute news show on a daily basis? By June, many of them had decided they needed an unannounced vacation day. Those staffers who did show up at NPR wound up pulling tapes at random to fill the airtime.

"We had some people who were literally right off the street and rookies who had never done radio before," says Susan Stamberg, who joined NPR in 1972 and went on to become The Voice of "ATC." "The very earliest years were a whole lot sloppier. If you listen to some of the early tapes, it was much more uneven. But when you invent something it's never going to be across-the-board terrific.

"There was always a handful of superb workers," she adds. "Always."

In many ways Siemering benefited from NPR's sidekick status, because the network could hide in the shadows while he worked out the kinks. "I knew it would take time to develop," he says.

A few months into the program, he decided to tinker with his host lineup. Conley had impeccable credentials as a journalist, but he lacked the approach-

able tone Siemering wanted for the show. One old-timer bluntly states that Conley was "boring."

Another hard-core newsman, Jim Russell from United Press International, took over the first hour of the broadcast, which focused on more traditional news coverage. Mike Waters followed with a thirty-minute soft-feature section. The two hosts never worked as a unit, so "ATC" aired like two separate shows. Russell burned out after just a few months. "He had nothing like the support he needed to do that show. He said, 'I don't want to do this,'" Waters recalls.

A young part-time staffer auditioned for the job. Siemering knew immediately that he'd found the voice he'd been looking for: part mom, part friend, part understanding, part laugh. "I said we needed a conversational tone, and Susan Stamberg's voice exemplified that. She's authentic. She's the same on as she is off the air. She's not afraid to ask the questions the listeners would ask. She just had this presence."

"We invented a way to speak to people," Stamberg says. "It's much more conversational and embracing, which was Bill's vision. We should talk in normal voices, and in me he found the way to do that." Waters and Stamberg became a team, and the show became one seamless, ninety-minute program.

Over the years, Stamberg and her cohost—first Waters, then Bob Edwards, and later Sanford Unger—tried to humanize "ATC" by sponsoring contests. They asked listeners, Why is April the cruelest month? The winner got May. When Chinese Vice Premier Deng Xiaoping came to the United States in 1979,

"I knew it would take time to develop," said Bill Siemering about "All Things Considered," and it did. Choosing hosts, finding a tone, defining the right chemistry were all tough. Hosts Robert Conley (opposite page, left) and Jim Russell (opposite page, right), both excellent print reporters, didn't work out. However, science reporter Ira Flatow (left) and Bob Edwards attracted a large audience immediately.

Alex Chadwick (right), who began his radio career on a commercial station in Brunswick, Maine, and a young Scott Simon (opposite), then NPR bureau chief in Chicago, both developed later into main attractions in Washington. Their styles seemed to fit what the stations and listeners wanted.

they described his official travel itinerary and told the audience to come up with an alternative. Some suggestions: Billy Carter's service station in Plains, Georgia; Al's Breakfast in Minneapolis; Harlem and Barbara Efie's house in San Francisco for carrot cake.

"All Things Considered" quickly developed a cultlike following of 4 to 5 million listeners. They knit mittens for Stamberg's little boy or sent her chicken soup when she sounded sick. She got marriage proposals and postcards from fans vacationing around the world. She had created a hometown radio station on a national scale.

And that same caring audience slapped their collective faces in shock when a photo of Susan Stamberg and then "ATC" cohost Bob Edwards appeared in a 1979 issue of *Time* magazine. One stunned couple wrote:

> Dear Ms. Stamberg and Mr. Edwards:
> We feel you should be informed that two imposters claiming to be Susan Stamberg and Bob Edwards are pictured in the current issue of *Time* magazine.
> As regular listeners of "All Things Considered" we know perfectly well that the calm, soothing, resonant voices which utter the mature wit and wisdom we enjoy so much do not emanate from such obviously youthful—indeed teenage-looking—frauds.
>
> Sincerely,
> Robert Paul Jones and Kay Jones
> *Kenosha, Wisconsin*

Sound protected the hosts from their own youth the way the printed word shields a young writer. The fact that listeners could only hear Stamberg, Edwards, and all the other popular NPR reporters meant that twenty-five-year-olds could be given key jobs and no one would have to worry about looking professional. Fans could paint the face of their choice on the voices they loved. The average "ATC" staffer was about twenty-six.

The network never could have carved out such an entirely new concept for radio programming if it hadn't hired so many fresh eyes. It needed people willing to take an unabashed look at an old sound medium.

"People at NPR at the time were always wondering, 'So what am I going to do when I grow up? When am I going to get a real job?'" says Alex Chadwick, who started at NPR in the mid-1970s after working as a radio reporter for a small commercial station in Brunswick, Maine. "It seemed like a great adventure, a great enterprise. Almost like being in combined elements of amateur theatrical productions and journalism. That kind of enthusiasm—'things are really going great.' But those things never last."

So the Beat poet in San Francisco got as much airtime as the utterings of a head of state. The line between news and cultural programming became very fine, at times, nonexistent. "All Things Considered" worked like a mesh net that entwined the doctor, the drug addict, the Iowa farmer, and the president all in one newscast. It got to the point where Susan Stamberg and science reporter Ira Flatow could broadcast "ATC" from a dark closet while they tested whether a Wint-O-Green Life Saver did indeed spark in the dark when chewed. It did. Their fans loved it.

"All Things Considered" also aired some very serious, path-breaking stories. One broadcast by Scott Simon, then a young bureau chief in Chicago, captures the luxuriously layered quality that NPR had achieved in its best work by the late 1970s.

Twenty Nazis wanted to gather at Chicago's Marquette Park, but an irate

Before Bob Edwards, Mike Waters (above) joined Susan Stamberg on "ATC." The program became a permanent part of the daily programming, although station managers still complained about it because, among other things, it "didn't sound like CBS."

crowd brought 1,500 police to the scene. With the sound of protesters howling in the background, Simon honed in on a man digging in his garden. The reporter wanted his opinion on the tension between the Nazis and the crowd. "I don't give a damn if they kill one another," the man said, as he continued to chop, chop, chop the soil. The sound of his spade became the news.

Then Simon turned his tape recorder to a young black girl singing a southern folk tune on a stoop. Angry men screamed behind her. The piece became a study in the contrasting sounds of humanity: a reassuring voice telling patients at a hospital for the elderly that everything would be okay, a helicopter drowning out the comforting tones.

By the time Simon's story aired in 1978, Siemering was long gone. The man who had fit together pieces from his work at stations in Wisconsin and Buffalo to create a new kind of public radio had been fired after just two years on the job.

During the first year, most of the member stations were preoccupied with survival. Of the 427 educational and community stations in existence in 1970—the year NPR incorporated—only 73 met the Corporation for Public Broadcasting's requirements for government funding. Al Hulsen, CPB's first director of radio, didn't want stations with no full-time staffers and sub-$10,000 budgets draining government support from stations that could air programming at least eighteen hours a day, six days a week. He knew CPB could never develop a legitimate radio network if it allowed every creaky jalopy to join the parade. The station managers fought the requirements but were unsuccessful.

When "ATC" aired in 1971, 104 stations in thirty-four states and Puerto Rico had scraped together the resources and full-time staffers necessary to qualify for NPR feeds. A few quiet months passed while everyone got their bearings, but then the complaints started coming in.

At the first station managers' conference in 1971, people came up to Siemering and told him his show "didn't sound like CBS." They wanted to know where the stars were and why he kept putting women on the air. "You know, these women's voices just don't carry on our transmitters," several of them said. "They just don't have a sound of authority." They didn't like the eclectic music selection or the folksy, offbeat "news" pieces. They wondered aloud why NPR had chosen to launch a news show in the afternoon instead of the morning, when the listening audience is larger.

"I remember the manager of WETA [Washington, D.C.'s public radio station] coming up to me in the fall and saying, 'Look, we're going to take this off the air,'" says Siemering. "'It's not measuring up to our standards. It doesn't sound good—too amateurish. If there's not improvement in two months, it's gone.' Imagine if we had lost Washington," he says with a dark laugh. "That wouldn't have been good."

Ironically, NPR had been stationed in Washington, D.C., in part because the founders wanted to get away from the New York media circus. They wanted a network with a more varied, cross-country, East-to-West take on America. Now WETA wanted to pull "ATC" because it didn't fit the New York mold.

The station managers just couldn't adjust to this new animal. Clearly it wasn't commercial radio. It certainly wasn't land-grant educational radio. NPR had become some kind of unrecognizable hybrid. They didn't know what to do with it.

NPR management also went on the attack. When they asked Siemering which "ATC" staffers he wanted to bring to the next managers' conference, he said—everybody. "We were small," he explains. NPR President Don Quayle was not amused. Maybe next time Siemering will want to bring the janitor, one administrator chided.

The two sides couldn't even see eye-to-eye on simple things like job titles and dress codes. "They wanted to know what Mike Waters's title was," Siemering recalls. "And I said, 'Well, he's a first-rate editor and a great reporter. Why can't we just call him Mike Waters?' They went crazy with that kind of stuff."

As the station managers pressed in on the network, management became more concerned that Siemering look the part of a serious director. "I didn't look like a director of programming," he says. "I looked like a regular guy at the time. I might wear a crushed velvet tie, a striped shirt and a corduroy jacket."

Quayle says that he hired Siemering because Siemering wrote the mission statement for the net-work and "it sounded good on paper. But Bill is a poet and a philosopher, not a manager. I found the staff working around him and past him and not *for* him. He kept 'communing' with the staff instead of running it."

Jack Mitchell, producer for "All Things Con-sidered" at the time, found himself caught in the middle. "Quayle felt Bill was a wonderful philoso-pher and idea person and very inspirational but *not* a good organizer," he says. "I certainly saw that

"I didn't look like a director of programming," explains Bill Siemering. "I might wear a crushed velvet tie, a striped shirt, and a corduroy jacket." Whatever it was—clothes, style, or program-ming—Siemering departed in December 1972, barely two years after "ATC," largely his creation, went on the air.

and tried to fill the gap, but I didn't think Bill had to go." Oddly enough, Mitchell adds, the show had really hit its stride by the time Siemering got fired. "Maybe that's why action was taken against him," he conjectures. "As long as 'ATC' was evolving there were options, but once they'd honed in, well . . ."

Siemering received the news on a December day in 1972. Quayle called the director into his office and told him, "It's time for you to go." Siemering remembers the time of the meeting, the dialogue. He remembers that it was a Sunday.

"I had made some changes," he insists. "I had listened. But it was too late." Twenty years later, his grief can still fill a room.

Quayle reorganized after Siemering's departure by splitting the director's job into two divisions: news and cultural. Within the year, he left as well to become senior vice president of CPB's television division. The corporation and PBS were feuding viciously, and the new CPB president, John Macy, thought Quayle could patch things up.

"I hated to go," he says. "I was having the time of my life at NPR."

Siemering headed west to KCCM in Moorhead, Minnesota, after leaving NPR, and later he worked as vice president of programming at Minnesota Public Radio, one of the founding stations for NPR competitor American Public Radio. "I had a choice of just being in exile and angry about it all my life," he says, "or I could say 'Damn it!' and redeem myself. So I ran for [NPR's] board [of directors] as a petition candidate and got elected. I wound up serving more years than anybody."

He also left behind many of the staffers he'd hired and trained. They continued to shade the NPR canvas with Siemering-like strokes. Other top talent, including Bob Edwards, Neal Conan, and Robert Siegel, joined original staffers like Stamberg and Wertheimer. Together they embraced the new brand of public radio. As the NPR audience grew, station managers became more accustomed to their medium's new face.

But it took a man who had barely heard of NPR to bring the network into the big time: Frank Mankiewicz.

He grew up in Hollywood, where his father wrote scripts for movies, including Orson Welles's *Citizen Kane*. At the age of twenty-five he made a failed attempt to win a seat in the California legislature, then decided to work as a freelance journalist for a few years. He catapulted into national politics in the 1960s as Robert Kennedy's press secretary. His career continued to take brilliant twists and turns, from a job as campaign manager for George McGovern in the 1972 presidential campaign, to running NPR during the network's formative years. But when he looks back on it all, Mankiewicz still claims that the most charged moment of his life was when he had to go on national television and announce that Bobby Kennedy had been assassinated.

When NPR hired Mankiewicz as its president in 1977, the network had a distinctive style and a growing audience, but it remained "the best kept secret in journalism."

Producers Maury Schlesinger (left) and Walter Watson (above) give the newscasts coherence and flow.

NPR is an institution where women play important roles. Melissa Block (above), "ATC" senior producer, and Alice Furlaud (right), a commentator, are part of the mix.

"I was brought in to raise less corn and more hell," he says.

He knew artists from his California days. He knew Washington from his Kennedy and McGovern days. He was the contact man. The man with the huge Rolodex. "When I was interviewed for the job," Mankiewicz recalls, some people on the board asked me, 'If you get this job, what do you think would be your priority?' I said, 'To do whatever necessary so that people like me have heard of NPR.'"

Within a year the new president had scored a major coup. He fought and won the right to have NPR broadcast the Panama Canal Treaty debate live from the Senate floor. It marked the first time any network had aired the Senate in action. Not only had Mankiewicz gotten the story, but he had the guts to appoint a woman—Linda Wertheimer—as the anchor for the broadcast.

The media critics at *The New York Times* gave the coverage a rave review and said it could mark the beginning of a "renaissance" in radio programming. "Panama was our coming of age," Mankiewicz says.

He used NPR's growing credibility as leverage in his fight for more money. Radio generally received less than 10 percent of the total funds available for public broadcasting at CPB; Mankiewicz wanted and got 25 percent. With the additional money he drew in more talent and boosted the news department.

"Really talented people began coming in," says Stamberg. "We had been doing good work, but Mankiewicz was able to project that. He had the connections. We began surpassing anything that we were before that. It was quite amazing."

He hired Barbara Cohen, managing editor of *The Washington Star*, to head his news department, and he "discovered" congressional correspondent Cokie Roberts. The increased emphasis on news kept stars like Siegel, Conan, and Nina Totenberg from wandering off. NPR granted them airtime and editorial freedom they couldn't have found anywhere else in broadcasting—TV or radio.

While the network built up behind the scenes, Mankiewicz continued his public relations crusade. Stories on NPR plays, NPR music, NPR news started appearing everywhere. The network's audience nearly doubled from 4.5 million to 8.5 million listeners. NPR had moved from cult to mainstream.

A magical combination — Noah Adams and Susan Stamberg — brought "All Things Considered" an increasing and loyal audience. Listeners, a little sad when both left, cheered when they returned.

Despite the shift, "All Things Considered" managed to retain some of its trademark playfulness and unpredictability. Noah Adams could still get on the air with a story that featured his rock-and-roll version of "Always Been a Dreamer." He'd found a place that let people record their own rendition of a favorite pop song. The company provided the music and technical equipment. The customer provided the vocals. Adams decided to share his final take with the "ATC" audience.

"Take it [dramatic pause] to the limit everrrrrry time." For a man with a great radio voice, he sounded remarkably off-key.

"I have to tell you," he told cohost Susan Stamberg, "there was this moment, during about the fifteenth take, even though I was really embarrassed, that I was actually enjoying it. I sort of felt that I *could* really be a rock-and-roll singer."

"Oh, how lucky you are to have had that experience," Stamberg said with an audio smirk. "And how *brave* you are to have shared it with us."

In *Every Night at Five: Susan Stamberg's All Things Considered Book*, Stamberg recalls another equally playful newscast that Adams did while hosting "All Things Considered Weekend Edition" in 1978. He and his cohost, Jackie Judd, invited listeners to name and defend their favorite hamburgers. Adams had gotten the idea for the story after reading Calvin Trillin's *American Fried*. The author went on the air with his response: "I made a firm decision about where the best hamburger in the world was when I was fourteen and naturally haven't changed my mind. I think anybody who changes his mind after the age of fourteen on a matter like that is a deviate, a backslider, a security risk."

> People at NPR at the time were always wondering, 'So what am I going to do when I grow up? When am I going to get a real job?' It seemed like a great adventure, a great enterprise. Almost like being in combined elements of amateur theatrical productions and journalism.
> —*Alex Chadwick, NPR reporter*

Adams then inquired, "If I came to New York and asked for a good place to get a hamburger, what would you tell me?"

"I would tell you to fly to Kansas City," responded Trillin.

The sound quality of NPR programming took a quantum leap the following year when it switched to a satellite distribution system—the first of its kind in the country. Before 1979 the member stations received the network's feeds from a single, five-kilohertz monaural line, which worked little better than a souped-up telephone.

"We had one channel. Period," says Ralph Woods, current manager of satellite operations. NPR could only offer one program at a time. Everything else, including *all* music, had to go through the mail, a process the industry calls "bicycling tapes." So the live concert in Vienna became the week-old concert for listeners in Seattle.

The satellite gave NPR a minimum of four channels (now twelve), which meant it could broadcast a hearing, a jazz concert from New Orleans, and a play simultaneously; and the 218 member stations could take their pick or just tape all the material and run it when they chose. The tonal quality also improved drastically. Susan Stamberg and her colleagues on "ATC" stopped sounding like the neighbor on the phone and started sounding like they were actually in the room.

At the time, Mankiewicz joked with reporters from *The Washington Post* and said that he'd told the engineers to "add some static to make it credible. People will have trouble, at first, believing it's a live transmission. I used to know a mess sergeant who would crush ping-pong balls and put them in the powdered eggs. It's the same artistic principle."

Even with the satellite and the talent and the vision, NPR probably never would have found a seat at the table with big-time media if Mankiewicz hadn't also secured the money necessary to launch a morning news show. The birth of "Morning Edition" in 1979 transformed NPR into a full-fledged news organization. The network entered the 1980s with the flush feeling that it had become so much more than an "amateur theatrical production" with journalistic tendencies. It had evolved into America's primary source for high-quality radio.

Playful and unpredictable moments are a trademark of NPR. From Noah Adams doing his own on-air rock-and-roll version of "Always Been a Dreamer" to an interview about hamburgers with author Calvin Trillin (right), each one adds some new dimension to the ability of sound alone to convey a feeling, an emotion, or a bit of information.

CHAPTER FOUR

The "Morning Edition"

If more people listen to the radio in the morning than at any other time of the day, why did NPR put "All Things Considered" in the afternoon? Well, it appears that no one wanted to work the night shift. "When you're creating new things you really need people working daylight hours," says Bill Siemering.

"Can you believe that?" says Alex Chadwick, still incredulous more than a decade later. "It was completely stupid in terms of radio. Dumb as hell."

NPR didn't have the cash for an overnight staff anyway, but its laissez-faire approach to the problem said volumes about its priorities. Fewer than half of the member stations even went on the air in the morning because they had nothing to broadcast. Managers complained, but Siemering had conceived of a lengthy, essaylike show that just didn't mesh with people's need for traffic reports, news updates, and the time in the morning. NPR's programming mission took precedence over member stations' immediate needs.

The network did throw out a bone—a nine-minute morning program called "A Closer Look," which followed short newscasts on the hour from 7:00 a.m. to 9:00 a.m. "It was sort of nothing," says Chadwick, who got his start at NPR as a host for that show.

"Before we had a job as a weekend part-time librarian, I think that was about as low as you could enter on the air," says Robert Siegel, another "Closer Look" veteran.

The whole setup was reminiscent of the days in 1936 when Ed Bliss, former newswriter for Edward R. Murrow and Walter Cronkite, used to just pop in to a radio studio in Columbus, Ohio, and read a script for about fifteen minutes, then get off the air. No staff. No prescription from management on what the show should do. "They just wanted it taken care of," says Chadwick.

During one broadcast, Chadwick devoted the entire nine minutes to a baseball game. The Pittsburgh Pirates and Chicago White Sox had racked up the second highest score in the history of professional baseball, 22 to 21, in fifteen innings of play. Chadwick called Chicago newspaper columnist Mike Royko, and they chatted about what it must feel like to lose a game after scoring twenty-one runs. Chadwick concedes, "It was dumb."

But as 1973 gave way to 1974 and then 1975, it began to dawn on NPR staff and management that maybe "they really would keep going," he says. Maybe they all had real jobs after all. Which, of course, meant that the network had to start taking the morning show problem more seriously. By the time

Mankiewicz arrived in 1977, it had become NPR's top priority. "I knew that as long as all they had was one news show in the afternoon that it wouldn't be enough," says Mankiewicz. "I always thought that if you had a program in the morning and one in the afternoon that people would leave their radio on that part of the dial."

He began working with programming director Sam Holt. Together they built a show in their heads "before we even had a nickel to put it on the air," he says. A byzantine twist in public broadcasting politics eventually got them the cash they needed.

The Corporation for Public Broadcasting had no time for radio. From CPB's point of view, NPR was nothing more than a sound blip in a visual era. Nothing that the network could conjure up could possibly be worth a multimillion-dollar investment.

But then President Richard Nixon unintentionally came to the rescue like a black knight on a white horse. He hated the media. In particular he hated public broadcasting, because it spent tax dollars on programs that dealt with hot social and political topics. He refused to sign a 1972 appropriations bill that would have finally resolved CPB's long-range funding woes. Since Congress couldn't garner enough votes to override the veto, public broadcasting was left, once again, with just enough money for one fiscal year.

Public television gave in to the political pressure and dropped several spirited shows like "Firing Line" and "Washington Week in Review." But the skittish public broadcasting system wasn't sure if even that was enough. By 1973, CPB President John Macy "had decided that the Nixon administration wouldn't be forthcoming with prominent Democrats in top positions, so he resigned," says Don Quayle, NPR's first president. "Henry Loomis came on as president."

Nixon seemed victorious. He had "his" man in now—a Yankee Republican who had headed the Voice of America. But then the Watergate scandal broke, and both NPR and PBS began airing the hearings. Peeved, Nixon refused to act on the most recent long-range funding bill for public broadcasting. It sat on his desk untouched. As he neared his zero hour, his staff tried to convince him that short-changing public broadcasting at this juncture would surely be viewed as vindictive. He finally relented and signed the legislation into law in July 1974. By August, he had resigned from office.

But Loomis remained. And, as fate would have it, he was a true radio fan. "Henry is the last president of CPB, as far as I know, that I heard use the word *radio*," says Mankiewicz.

Alex Chadwick, having coffee with Lynn Neary (opposite page), was one of the people who struggled devotedly to define "Morning Edition." News director Barbara Cohen (above left with Frank Mankiewicz at the 1980 Republican National Convention) and a young producer, Jay Kernis, were also there at the creation.

Loomis called Mankiewicz and told him: "You may not know this, but CPB gets all of its money on the first day of the fiscal year. Every other government agency gets its money as it spends it or periodically, but CPB gets the whole amount. So over the year we develop a considerable income from interest."

"Considerable" wound up being almost $4 million.

"What would you do if I gave you all the money?" Loomis asked.

"I'd start a morning news program," said Mankiewicz.

"That's a terrific idea!"

Bingo. And so "Morning Edition" was born.

Later when Loomis asked Mankiewicz how he planned to fund the new program the following year, the NPR president replied, "Blackmail."

"You're learning," laughed Loomis.

"See, I knew I could go to CPB and say, 'You want to be known for taking "Morning Edition" off the air?'" says Mankiewicz. "No way."

But his strategy would only work if NPR could create an irreplaceable program. So Mankiewicz formed a "Morning Edition" committee, complete with news director Barbara Cohen; Alex Chadwick, host of "A Closer Look"; outside experts from the University of Maryland; psychiatrists (who told him what people "feel" when they wake up); and Jay Kernis, a relatively new producer who had worked on a weekly arts program, "Voices in the Wind."

Kernis started at NPR in 1974 in the public relations department, where he produced thirty-second promotional tapes for upcoming shows or specials. During his two years at the job, he worked with every program, every host, every producer. "It was a great education," he says. "I learned how to write for the audience, how to respect the intelligence of that audience. Every promo had

Before the words there is the melody. Composer B. J. Liederman (right) gave "Morning Edition" a distinctive musical theme that gently wakes NPR listeners and leads them into another day. But words matter, too. Commentators add depth and breadth to NPR. Rod MacLeish (opposite page) added even more to "Morning Edition" —a distinguished literary style.

to say that this is a place where we have fun and explore the length and breadth of life. I did it for classical music programs, cultural programs, news, etc. It also taught me how to be disciplined with time. I had to do everything in thirty seconds."

Kernis eventually shifted to "Voices in the Wind" as an assistant producer, then worked his way up to producer. But when NPR decided to put "Morning Edition" on the air in 1979, it cut the arts program to save money. That summer Kernis found himself locked in a room with all the other morning show committee members brainstorming ideas for a format, theme, and hosts.

He became the king of pie charts. Station managers would tell the committee what kind of structure they wanted, and Kernis would go home and draw up a diagram that reflected their suggestions: five-minute newscast, followed by a break for local stations to come in, then a nine-minute story from NPR, then another break. A cutaway here, a story there. They tinkered until Kernis had drawn the perfect circle of time for a two-hour morning show.

"I hated it," says Chadwick. "All these consultants, like Larry Lichty from the University of Maryland, kept saying that we had to make the program user-friendly for the member stations so that they can get in and out, but it was a cookie-cutter approach to programming."

Kernis agrees that from a producer's point of view the show seemed repetitious and choppy, but "we had to create it so people could use it.

"We were told by the stations that 'Morning Edition' had to be a service," he says. "The morning program has more of a local function, very little national function. Stations had to be able to move in and out so they could give people the traffic, weather, etc. So we came up with the dump and join."

Actually the idea was hardly new. NBC used a similar approach on Monitor Radio, and ABC had experimented with a twenty-four-hour news service that stations could cut in and out of whenever they wanted. CBS also had a national feed, but no one had created a regular morning radio program. Kernis's unusual hybrid creation would work both as a news service and a complete show.

In his spare time, Kernis had established himself as a professional collage artist. Now he had to take those cut-and-paste skills and fuse them with the sense of timing he had gained from his stint in the network's PR department. As he himself admits, it was probably a good thing he never presented himself as a newsman, or the show might have become just another dry news service with lengthier stories. He managed to incorporate "culture, history, and human character" into the content proposal for the show.

Even Alex Chadwick softened: "I thought what was important was all the intelligence and spontaneity we brought to what we were doing at NPR. I thought all that would be stamped out by this structure, but it wasn't. So Jay became an ally of mine and an ally of Lichty's as well."

So "Morning Edition" had money and a format. All it needed was a staff. Mankiewicz hired some producers from commercial radio and two hosts—Mary Tillotson, now with CNN, and Pete Williams, who later served as spokesman for the Pentagon during the Gulf War. They did a couple of pilot programs that smelled of bubble gum.

Everything seemed a bit too perky, a bit too commercial—the voices, the music, the story selection. One feature began with Tillotson asking in a cheery, TV-morning-show voice, "Have you ever had a sty in your eye? It makes my eyes water just to talk about it." Then a break to a man in Buffalo, New York, commenting about styes in his eyes. "What to do?" Tillotson asks. "This is what the doctors say. It's very tricky. . . ."

I hate to get up in the morning. Please don't make me get up in the morning. Let me stay in bed . . . and sleep.
—Alleged lyrics to the "Morning Edition" theme song by B. J. Liederman

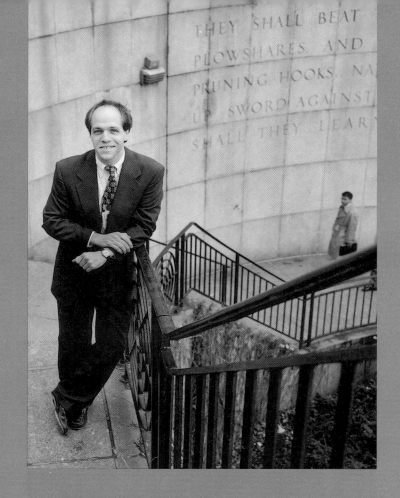

The psychiatrists that Mankiewicz hired told him that the first feeling that most people have when they wake up "is a sense of relief. 'Wow, I made it one more time.' Then you look for security." And get—a cheery piece on styes in your eye.

The pilot bombed with the stations. Chadwick says the managers agreed: "Great music. Great format. Great idea. But lousy radio program."

"Susan and I laughed after listening to the pilot," says Bob Edwards. "It cracked us up, because that was our potential in-house competition, and we just said, 'Ha, the show's over. Got no problem here.'" He blames the producers rather than Tillotson and Williams for the failure, because the hosts just aired what their bosses wanted, he says.

Two weeks before the scheduled debut of "Morning Edition," Mankiewicz fired all four people he had hired for the show. He handed the reins to the most senior staffer left: Jay Kernis, who went back to his collage and, in his own words, "sort of reinvented the show in one night."

"Mankiewicz said, 'Okay, Kernis, you're the one who sort of designed the show with all these pie charts, now produce it.' But implicit in his expression was 'If you ever embarrass me, I'll never forgive you.'"

To give the program a more cultured, intelligent tone, Kernis pulled together many of the staffers left dangling after several arts and entertainment programs, including "Folk Festival USA" and "Voices in the Wind," had been dropped so NPR could weather the financial strain of launching "Morning Edition." Then he began poking around for a host and settled on Bob Edwards. "I didn't think Susan would ever leave 'All Things Considered,'" Kernis says, "but I thought if we asked for Bob on a temporary basis they might let me have him. And one executive at the table said, 'Never. He could never leave "ATC."'"

Ultimately, NPR news programs depend on the quality of the reporting by skilled and fair-minded people such as (opposite, clockwise from top left) Jim Zarroli, Phyllis Crockett, Sunni Khalid, Katie Davis, and (above) Ted Clark.

But Mankiewicz agreed immediately: "He would have always been a second banana to Susan. I think he welcomed the chance. When people thought of 'ATC,' they didn't think of Bob Edwards, they thought of Susan." Besides, he adds, there had always been some tension between the chatty Stamberg and the more sedate Edwards—though both hosts deny that. Edwards had sat in her spotlight for five years. Now he could have his own show.

"I had wonderful years with her, but that was really her program. It was a challenge to see if we could make the morning show as successful as 'All Things Considered,'" Edwards says.

He signed on for a thirty-day trial run and has stayed for thirteen years.

He remembers having to make a conscious shift in his delivery. "The engineer said I needed to gun it up about 60 percent from where I was. They thought I was too laid back on 'ATC,' so I purposely put a little more umph into it.

"To a commercial radio person, if you listen to 'Morning Edition' you would not think this program moves along. But moving from 'ATC' to 'Morning Edition'—then you think, well, this thing really motors."

He actually began the show with a cohost, Barbara Hockner; but she left within months, and Edwards decided to go it alone. "I felt more freedom to do what I wanted to do, to be who I wanted to be," he says. "Actually, I really have 400 cohosts because of the shared format. Each of the local stations assigns someone, so why do I need someone else here? I think, inadvertently, I've done a lot for hiring women for local newscasts because I'm a guy, and they like the male/female combination."

The stations began signing on in droves. Finally, a user-friendly, service-oriented public radio program. But Edwards's departure proved a heavy blow to "ATC." When asked if the NPR news staff resented the shift, Mankiewicz says, "Naah."

"He's wrong," retorts Stamberg. "He wasn't behind the scenes, behind the microphone." From her perspective the change proved an unmitigated disaster. "All Things Considered" began hemorrhaging as the morning news program siphoned off not only Edwards but reporters and other support staff.

Cokie Roberts (opposite) listened in when party chairman Lee Atwater called George Bush from the 1988 Republican National Convention. Foreign correspondent Anne Garrels (left) has also hosted "Morning Edition." Bob Edwards (below) entertains a prime audience at home.

"It was awful, just awful," she says. "I went a whole year without a permanent cohost. And in those days the host carried that program. The work load had already been so enormous with two of us. It became a revolving door of substitutes.

"People who heard 'All Things Considered' and had a connection with me didn't like the fact that I was hanging around with all these different men." She laughs. "'You're sounding fickle on the air,' they said. It wasn't until Noah [Adams] came that I was able to work it out.

"I realize it had to happen. . . ." Her voice trails off. She and others sense that the birth of "Morning Edition" completely altered the direction of NPR. The network had to establish a presence during radio's peak listening hours; but the fact that the show wound up so service-oriented, so much faster, and had such stature so quickly that even the flagship show "All Things Considered" had to make sacrifices on its behalf, proved that NPR had stepped into a new era. Mankiewicz had placed the bow of the ship smack in the middle of the mainstream.

NPR staffers tried to fight the more geared-up approach. According to former news director Barbara Cohen, the cheery announcement that they would now have to double their output received a "hostile" response.

"They lied," says longtime correspondent Cokie Roberts with a knowing laugh. "They told us that we really wouldn't be doing very much for it, that

we'd be writing a news spot here and there. That it was really a host's show.

"They knew they'd have us over a barrel in the end, because they had these statistics that showed us that morning is when most people like to listen to the radio. And they knew that all of us were egomaniacal enough that once we found out that everyone was listening, we'd want to be on that program. And right they were."

Kernis's finished product finally hit the airwaves in November 1979: "Good morning. Today is Guy Fawkes Day. Guy's plot to blow up the parliament was discovered on this day in 1605. Today is the beginning of National Split Pea Soup Week and the debut of this program. I'm Bob Edwards."

And this is a new NPR.

Mankiewicz remembers riding in a taxi in Chicago when he heard the premiere broadcast. The show was about fifteen minutes old. "Hey, my God," he told the cabbie, "that's the program — 'Morning Edition' on NPR."

"Yeah," replied the driver. "I always listen to it."

CHAPTER FIVE

Early Sound Portraits

News made NPR, but the network needed first-rate cultural programming if it ever hoped to fulfill Bill Siemering's mandate that public radio become an aural museum. It took some brilliant steps in that direction during the 1970s and early 1980s with weekly programs like "Jazz Alive" and specials like "Father Cares: The Last of Jonestown"; but those flashes tended to be the exception, not the rule.

NPR never quite pieced together a full-fledged arts and performance division that could send out a considerable volume of high-quality programs. The critics oohed and aahed at practically everything the network did in drama, music, and specials, because the American airwaves had almost nothing like it. A simple comparison between England's BBC, which often aired a thousand hours of radio drama a year, and NPR, which rarely produced more than fifty, underscores just how far American radio lagged behind its European counterparts in the field of arts and entertainment.

"We were not able to produce very much," says Joe Gwathmey, a former vice president for programming. "My recollection was that we were heavily dependent on what others could supply us."

A handful of extraordinary producers did manage to create a limited but extremely influential body of work. As former NPR music specialist Frederica Kushner points out, it's the producers who usually "conceive of the program or piece, who write the script, obtain the actors, do the interviews, edit the tape, and work with engineers on the final mix. In many instances the producer *is* the program." Listeners may be more likely to remember a host's voice or a particular musical theme, but it's the producer's name that really belongs at the bottom of the canvas.

Robert Montiegel surely stands out as one of the grand masters of the early period. Some call him an "absolute genius"; others describe him as "very, very difficult—very exacting." All agree that he used sound in astounding new ways to produce programs that remain some of NPR's best. At his funeral in 1992, former coworkers like Noah Adams, Frank Mankiewicz, and Jay Kernis put on a farewell show complete with excerpts from Montiegel's work and a poetry reading.

The title of perhaps his greatest work, "A Question of Place," hangs in NPR's main conference room, surrounded by drawings of the twelve twentieth-century thinkers and writers that he featured in that series: Bertolt Brecht,

A landmark cultural event on NPR, "A Question of Place," produced by Robert Montiegel, featured the lives and work of twelve disparate intellectuals, including James Joyce (right), Bertolt Brecht, William Faulkner, and W.E.B. Du Bois.

Noam Chomsky, Simone de Beauvoir, W. E. B. Du Bois, William Faulkner, Michel Foucault, Sigmund Freud, Robert Frost, James Joyce, Claude Levi-Strauss, Bertrand Russell, and Igor Stravinsky.

"The original idea was to do a kind of intellectual history of the twentieth century, to identify who the seminal thinkers had been, regardless of discipline; people who had contributed to the modern understanding of the world," says Mary Lou Finnegan, who worked with Montiegel on the thirteen-part series, which aired in 1980.

A panel of scholars haggled over who should be profiled—James Joyce or Mark Twain? Jung or Freud? "There were boxes and boxes of files that were the minutes of their deliberations," she says. Once they settled on a list, Montiegel had to find specialists capable of leaving the ivory tower and playing with radio. He wanted something more than just a scholarly paper for the airwaves. "We didn't want to have a paper script which we then just recorded," Finnegan says. "We wanted to build the program out of the sound that we got."

The final sound portraits marked a stunning excursion into a new kind of radio in America. The one-hour episode on James Joyce, possibly the best of the collection, captures the Irish author's ear for the language so effectively it makes one wonder why English departments don't always require students to read Joyce's work aloud.

What better way to truly feel the sensuality of Molly Bloom in *Ulysses* than to have a husky-voiced Irish actress read Molly's orgasmic close:

> . . . how he kissed me under the Moorish wall and I thought well as well him as another and then I asked him with my eyes to ask again yes and then he asked me would I yes to say yes my mountain flower and first I put my arms around him yes and drew him down to me so he could feel my breasts all perfume yes and his heart was going like mad and yes I said yes I will Yes.

The audio version makes it a bit easier to grasp why the United States banned the book for years.

Such dramatizations make up just one part of the hour-long broadcast. Montiegel layered the program with music from the period, comments from Joyce's contemporaries, and scholars' views on the author's fiction. Throughout the program, Irish announcer Terrance Courier repeats, "Great minds are very near to madness," a line from Joyce's short story "Grace." In many ways it became the mantra for the series as a whole, as episode after episode explored the tenuous border many of these thinkers walked as they sought beauty in their work or mind-altering insights.

At his funeral service in 1992, Montiegel was eulogized as the creator of extraordinary cultural programming, a genius who made "radio with a microphone, not a pen" a guiding principle.

Much of what Montiegel perfected in this series he had already tried on an earlier weekly program, "Voices in the Wind." Launched in 1974, the show promised to "report on the creative arts experience in the contemporary world." That included interviews with actors, poets, sculptors, painters, and others who didn't always have fifteen minutes worth of something to say. The program could have used a good editor, but as a museum piece it does offer insight into the early stages of Montiegel's artistic development.

Both Mary Lou Finnegan and Jay Kernis agree that NPR producers, including Montiegel, turned to Germany in the 1970s and early 1980s for insights on how to use sound more creatively on

radio. Peter Leonhard Braun from Sender Freies Berlin refined a revolutionary approach that used pure sound to tell a story in his documentary "The Bells of Europe." The piece followed the history of the famous bells of Europe that were melted down to make cannons during World War II, then recast after the war. Using simple narration and the pealing bells, Braun told a tale of death and rebirth. Kernis says that when Robert Siegel heard the tape, he decided to send several NPR producers to Europe to study with Braun. "A Question of Place" marked the first time an American radio program successfully imitated the German model by producing "radio with a microphone, not a pen," says Finnegan.

The following year, NPR used the same layered approach in "Father Cares: The Last of Jonestown," a ninety-minute special on the mass suicide of 913 men, women, and children who followed preacher Jim Jones into the Guyana wilderness. Instead of exploring the beauty of words and discovery, the program plunged into the bestiality of human nature. The piece is so dark, so disturbing, that an aural museum would surely have to post a warning sign and perhaps even run the tape in a cordoned-off room. "It's an amazing portrait of insanity and megalomania," said Barbara Cohen, who was director of NPR news at the time and is now with CBS.

While researching a book on the mass suicide, author James Reston, Jr., stumbled on 900 hours of tapes that Jones had recorded of his activities with his followers. The voice that had lured 913 victims to Guyana, that had taken away their ability to think for themselves, could now be heard by radio listeners across America.

"Father Cares: The Last of Jonestown" was called "the best radio ever put on the air." Created by writer James Reston, Jr. (above), producer Deborah Amos (inset upper right), and host Noah Adams (inset lower right), the show captured the frenzy of the mass suicide in an open-air church in Guyana (opposite).

Producer Deborah Amos, host and writer Noah Adams, and Reston worked together to cull telling excerpts for a documentary that would "go a long way towards explaining the mystery of mass suicide and certainly the man behind the event," said Cohen. Only radio could have captured the hypnotic nature of Jones's crusade: no visuals, no print, just sound.

The program opens with the voice of a black woman singing a spiritual: "I never heard a man speak this way before." People clap behind her as her voice gains momentum. Suddenly the tape cuts to a boy telling a crowd that he is ready to die if Father Jones wants him to. They cheer.

"Perhaps Father was evil, even bestial from the beginning," host Noah Adams says at one point during the program. His gentle, hushed tones serve as

a calming influence as the frenzy of Jones's mission unfolds. "But he was surely bold and exciting with an animal sexuality. His voice was captivating. His presence was overwhelming."

The tapes Reston discovered record what Jones and his followers came to call "White Nights," during which Jones would work the crowd into a frenzy and ask them again and again if they were willing to die to prevent being captured by fascists, ready to die for socialism, ready to die for him. Yes, yes, yes, the followers would say; but unlike Molly Bloom, they embraced something that promised to destroy, rather than create, life.

The demonic quality of Jones's recordings so concerned the network that it set up a call-in with Bill Moyers as moderator after the show. "Psychiatrists said that it would be important that people have someone to talk to," says Frank Mankiewicz.

Anthony Lewis of *The New York Times* called

When others thought it couldn't be done, Karl Schmidt brought radio drama to the air on "Earplay," attracting major writing and acting talent to the series.

the documentary "the best radio ever put on the air."

By 1981 NPR had made an impact with another kind of drama: radio plays. When the network launched the weekly series "Earplay" a decade earlier, it consisted largely of vignettes for rush-hour commuters. Working out of the University of Wisconsin, host and producer Karl Schmidt continued to build the program until it aired 26 one-hour shows each year. He often relied on recycled short stories or novels, but during its heyday, "Earplay" attracted writing talent like Edward Albee, Archibald MacLeish, and John Irving, and acting talent like Meryl Streep, Len Cariou, and Fritz Weaver. Two of the plays—"Wings" by Arthur Kopit and "The Water Engine" by David Mamet—actually made it to Broadway.

Reviews ranged from slap-happy, because the critics couldn't believe anyone would even try to put radio drama on the air in the 1970s, to the more even-handed claim that some of the work was excellent, but most of it was esoteric and often dull. *Newsweek* credited NPR with bringing radio drama back in all its glory, and *The New York Times* called it a class act. But the reviewer at the *Los Angeles Times* found "'Earplay' frustratingly inconsistent—running a gamut of extremes that range from high-style originality to impenetrable gibberish." He went on to acknowledge that it did provide a "valuable testing ground for playwrights young and old."

The Masterpiece Radio Theater grew out of the modest success of "Earplay." Leo Tolstoy's *Anna Karenina*, D. H. Lawrence's *Sons and Lovers*, Herman Melville's *Moby Dick*, and other classics were aired as part of a fifty-two week series for 217 stations. Most of these productions received rave reviews. Robert Montiegel got his hand in NPR's push for a renaissance in radio drama through "William Shakespeare: A Portrait in Sound," a forerunner of the portraits he went on to do for "A Question of Place."

Eventually NPR built up enough momentum in its drama programming to gamble on a huge project: "Star Wars." George Lucas gave the radio rights for his blockbuster story to KUSC, the station at the University of Southern California, his alma mater. The station worked with NPR, which in turn joined with the BBC and Minnesota Public Radio, to produce a series of broadcasts. The BBC had never invested in American radio before, but Lucas's movie had been an incredible success in 1977, convincing the British network that the show could hit gold again in 1981.

"'Star Wars' was part of the great leap forward that began in 1977," says Joe Gwathmey. "The BBC didn't become the partner everyone envisioned they would be, but they did lend credibility to the venture."

What NPR really needed, however, was money. Lucas handed over the radio rights for free; but costs for actors, sound technicians, script writers, and other behind-the-scenes staff, as well as promotion and distribution, quickly overran the projected $150,000 budget.

Using the movie's original sound track and sound effects, producer Tom Voegeli of Minnesota Public Radio managed to pull together thirteen half-hour episodes based on an original script that centered around Luke Skywalker's pre-Star Wars years. Stations ran the special in conjunction with their fund-raising efforts.

Bill Kling, Minnesota Public Radio's president and a critic of NPR's cultural efforts, joined with others to develop American Public Radio as an alternative distributor of programming, including "A Prairie Home Companion."

The show opened: "High among the rebel councils stands the royal house of the planet Alderaan, whose members had always supported the Old Republic before it was subverted and overthrown by the Empire. . . ." More than a million listeners tuned in to at least one episode.

Despite production costs, the project had enough support to carry it through the second part of the trilogy, "The Empire Strikes Back."

"But then '83 hit," says Gwathmey. "So they never finished the last third."

"Then '83 hit." It sounds like a tornado, and in a sense it was. NPR found itself in a financial tailspin that killed not only plans for "The Return of the Jedi" but practically every other cultural and entertainment program at the network.

Voegeli refused to give up on his project and turned to a newly created organization: American Public Radio. Bill Kling, president of Minnesota Public Radio, and managers from five other stations had expressed disappointment in NPR's cultural programming division for years and felt the member stations could be better served by a separate distribution network that specialized in arts and performance offerings. So they established APR, which produced nothing but bought other people's work and sold it to public stations. American Public Radio gained instant credibility when it offered Garrison Keillor's "A Prairie Home Companion," which Mankiewicz had rejected as too parochial. The show became the most popular program on radio.

Star Wars, *the film, became thirteen half-hour shows on NPR when George Lucas handed over the radio rights free, and more than one million listeners tuned in for one program or another. It was an other-worldly success.*

APR took to Voegeli's project immediately, but it didn't want to air the last part of the trilogy without the other two serials. NPR refused to give up the radio rights, so the series was never finished.

"Jazz Alive" and "The Sunday Show," NPR's five-hour cultural newsmagazine, also got sucked into the vortex of Tornado '83. Both shows became path breakers in their own right in the 1970s, though the contribution of "The Sunday Show" wasn't crystal clear at the time.

"Jazz Alive" sprang out of an earlier weekly music series, "Folk Festival USA," which producer Steve Rathe launched in 1974. Up to that point NPR had put together some rather sophisticated classical music and opera programming, but it hadn't branched into alternative forms. The network wanted Rathe to produce something "more comprehensive," he says. That involved touring the country to attend festivals featuring little known talent. In the end the show became an audio record of distinctly American musical traditions.

A slice: "Make sure you get your hand stamped so you can get back in," says a woman handing out tickets. A banjo takes over the air, then a Jews Harp, and finally a harmonica. Some guitarists sit under a tree discussing the strings on their instruments. A listener can taste the cotton candy and feel the straw sticking in the heat. A profile of blues pianist Big Chief Ellis follows, with excerpts from his early concerts and a short biographical sketch.

"To listen. To learn. To participate. To enjoy the dance, the ritual, the crafts," says the host. "To share in the richness of America's heritage. These are the reasons why people go to folk festivals."

Rathe soon learned they also went to listen to jazz. "It was our good fortune in 1976 to go to the New Orleans Jazz and Heritage Festival," he says, "which was the perfect sort of confluence of jazz and folk music. Jazz is, in fact, a kind of folk music in a scholarly form, and in New Orleans it's an indigenous and traditional music."

The NPR staff liked what it heard and returned the following year to record an Ella Fitzgerald performance. "Stevie Wonder was sitting in the audience for that event," Rathe recalls. "I'm standing backstage, when all of a sudden Stevie Wonder is tugging at my sleeve. 'Do you mind if I go up on the stage?' he says. And I'm incredulous and say, 'Do I mind? No. Do you mind if we record it?' And he said no.

"The next thing I knew I'm watching Ella sing 'You Are the Sunshine of My Life' and talking about the fact that Stevie Wonder had written it, when he comes up from behind her and responds

The sounds of jazz were too rarely heard on American radio until "Jazz Alive" with host Billy Taylor became part of NPR's cultural fare. Taylor, an accomplished pianist himself, also had a Ph.D. and a style that attracted stations and listeners.

with the second line. She was absolutely knocked out. The power of that performance was extraordinary. It later led to their collaboration on a record. Well, it gave us the perfect approach for the first show of the new series," which they called "Jazz Alive."

Rathe wanted something new because "Folk Festival USA" had begun to feel a bit stale, he says. The show had explored every vein of American folk music by the time it went off the air in 1979. "Jazz Alive" left Rathe with a platform that encouraged further discovery.

"Being at NPR in the mid-seventies was like being a kid in a candy store," says Rathe. "Management thought we ought to be doing it all, especially jazz because that was really reflective of our cultural mandate to explore America's distinctive assets and to present them. I never felt anything but support for what we were doing."

The selection of the urbane Billy Taylor as host of the series set the stage for a new kind of jazz presentation on radio. Before 1977 most stations treated jazz like an X-rated music form, complete with crass announcers and late-night airtime.

A sampling from a 1945 broadcast from the Plantation Club in Los Angeles:

Ernie "Bubbles" Whitman: Well, jiggle my nerves and call me shakey, if it ain't the dreamboat herself. . . . Delightful, delovely, deLena Horne!
Lena: Thanks, Ernie. That's a pretty red tie you are wearing.
Bubbles: Red tie? Oh that. That's just my tongue hanging out.

Of course, many big-city stations, like the one based at the Riverside Church in New York City, aired some serious specials on jazz music before and after 1945; but the music form had clearly not broken through all the seedy stereotypes.

Marian McPartland hit just the right note with listeners, beginning with a joint appearance with Billy Taylor and ending with her own series, "Marian McPartland's Piano Jazz."

It took an accomplished jazz musician with a Ph.D. to turn the famous phrase, "Jazz is America's classical music," into something any audience—black or white—could understand and appreciate. Billy Taylor took a much more sophisticated approach to the artists. He interviewed them about their work and provided serious commentary about their development. He helped give jazz credibility. Within a year "Jazz Alive" became NPR's number-one syndicated show and ranked third—behind "ATC" and "Morning Edition"—for total number of listeners.

"It paved the way for jazz on public radio," says Tim Owens, who stepped in as producer after Rathe left the show in 1978.

Fans popped up in unexpected places.

"If there was ever an indigenous art form, one that is special and peculiar to the United States, represents what we are as a country, I would say it's jazz. . . . vivid, alive, aggressive, innovative on the one hand and the severest form of self-discipline on the other." President Jimmy Carter's opening remarks at the White House Jazz Festival in 1979 marked the first time a president had ever publicly supported the art form. "Jazz Alive" aired a special two-hour excerpt from the all-night performance, which included the best musicians of the era: Eubie Blake, Mary Lou Williams, Clark Terry, George Benson, and Chick Corea to name a few. The president even got into the act with his own vocal rendition of "Salt Peanuts," accompanied by Dizzy Gillespie and Max Roach.

Such successes led to specials like "Marian McPartland's Piano Jazz" series, which opened with McPartland sitting alongside Billy Taylor in a storage room filled with pianos. They talked about jazz and improvised in a sea of baby grands.

But no matter how much Dizzy and his colleagues jammed and the people

Dizzy Gillespie and Max Roach played the White House with unexpected vocal help. When President Jimmy Carter asked Gillespie to play "Salt Peanuts," Gillespie agreed, but only if Carter would sing it. Carter did and NPR aired it on "Jazz Alive."

cheered, no one at NPR could afford to lose sight of the fact that most member stations catered to classical music listeners. Jazz, blues, and folk were all welcome flutters in the fabric, but the network had to create something big and permanent in the classic tradition. So it decided to shoot for the arts equivalent of "All Things Considered."

"I created MAP—the Music and Arts Project," says Sam Holt, vice president for programming in 1978. "The goal was to take existing contracts with orchestras and get them into this one coordinated effort using the satellite to move around the country." That way the local stations would provide most of the programming and NPR would just serve as a nerve center.

"But MAP was effectively shot down by the stations at a meeting in Boston," says Joe Gwathmey, because it offered music the local stations could pretty much get without NPR's help. "So it was back to the drawing board, and what emerged was 'The Sunday Show.' It was something different—a five-hour block of fine arts and produced almost entirely at NPR."

The network turned inward to current staffers and selected Deborah Jane Lamberton as producer and Andy Trudeau as music coordinator, but it looked outward to fill the crucial post of executive producer. It settled on David Ossman, who had worked with a comedy troupe called "Fireside Theater." "He was brought in to juice it up," says Trudeau.

Ossman began by looking for a host who could break out of the classical tradition of stuffed-shirt announcers. After a frustrating search, he settled on himself. As host and head honcho he tried to tackle the cumbersome five-hour format and clarify the show's ambiguous mandate. Management wanted "The Sunday Show" to have a three-hour segment that could stand apart from a second two-hour segment, but that could run as one block just in case a station wanted the whole package. It proved even more difficult to handle than to describe.

"This made it extremely difficult to conceive of the program from start to finish," says Lamberton. "What happened was that we ended up making two separate programs that somehow also had to hang together as a single five-hour show. It was an impossible situation. That was the first conceptual problem with 'The Sunday Show.'"

The second big problem concerned content. Everyone agreed they wanted an "ATC"-type arts newsmagazine, but Sam Holt felt the stations wanted a performance program that would be largely classical in nature. David Ossman felt he had been "hired to develop something more broadly cultural, that music would be 60 percent of the show, but we would deal with all the other cultures in America in the other 40 percent of the show. . . . I wanted the show to be about America, about the arts in this country and not about dead, white, European men."

The premiere broadcast in 1982 reflected the show's split personality. It began with a Beethoven piano sonata recorded at the Kennedy Center, shifted to a sound portrait of classical guitarist Andres Segovia, but also included an

"The Sunday Show," a five-hour fine arts production of NPR, dealt with music as well as other, sometimes offbeat, cultural areas. One show included ten bellringers from Washington's National Cathedral.

interview with Milton Berle, a report from the Humana Festival of New American Plays in Louisville, Kentucky, and a preview of a ten-bell concert from the National Cathedral in Washington, D.C.

A commentator provided a play-by-play for the bell-ringing piece. "Well they almost messed up there, but they were able to pull it back together," he said. "It looks like bell ringer number ten got back into line."

"It was a riot," says Lamberton. "These were the kinds of artistic things we were fighting for, and management just looked at us and rolled their eyes. They wanted something very conservative." They wanted dead, white, European men.

But Ossman continued to press his approach. He covered a man who whistled opera and devoted a sizable portion of one program to an organ at the

Oakland Paramount Theater. "The Sunday Show" became a kind of audio Sunday newspaper.

"It was sold to the system as a kind of new approach to classical music," says Andy Trudeau, "but they found that classical music was occupying what they felt was less and less of a percent of the show."

Then Ossman decided to do a special to mark the seventieth birthday of composer John Cage. They commissioned the artist to write a piece specifically for the broadcast. The "song" consisted of having five stations pull a record at random and play it. Cage then took the songs and mixed them. A commentator provided background on the composer to help give the fifteen-minute experiment some sort of context.

"We got it on the air and there it was—just fabulous," says Ossman. "Then we came off the air in Washington and were congratulating ourselves. Then John Bos [from cultural programming] called me into his office and said, 'You are fired.'"

"They never figured out the difference between accessible and smirky," says Holt. "It was the 'Saturday Night Live' crew versus the accessible arts generation. A show for aging children was not right for an NPR audience."

"He [Ossman] perceived a program from an artistic standpoint, and the management perceived it as a service to the stations," says Lamberton. "The greatest failing of NPR regarding 'The Sunday Show' was that management did not make a strong commitment to a show that would work. They tried to appease the requests of particular key stations—major market stations—and sometimes those requests were quite disparate. The bottom line is that it created a series of guidelines that were an anathema to the program's integrity."

> Public radio should be an aural museum — an available source of musical and literary masterpieces.
> —*Bill Siemering in "Public Radio: Some Essential Ingredients"*

The press plugged the show relentlessly with the same kind of desperate praise it had lauded on the "Earplay" series. Again, critics seemed simply grateful that NPR would even try to produce a national arts show. In 1983 it won a Peabody Award, one of radio's highest honors, for work in its 1982 season. No one invited David Ossman to the ceremony.

"The Sunday Show" died the year it received the award, a victim of its own inherent inconsistencies and NPR's consuming financial crisis. Its demise and the eventual gutting of the arts and entertainment division transformed NPR into a news-driven network once again. During the late 1970s and early 1980s management did try to make NPR a more viable and predictable presence as a provider of music and public affairs shows; but when the money got low, these tentative gains became mere shadows.

"The performance department was always struggling to find out what it was and to achieve parity with news," says Joe Gwathmey. "I think some very good ideas developed regarding a service that would present performance programming as seriously as politics or economics, but the idea was never realized. Regrettably most programs were weekly, even though NPR knew that listeners don't listen to programs but to stations. Conventional wisdom said that if a program wasn't on at a regular time on a regular basis, then it wasn't worth doing."

Even Frank Mankiewicz concedes that while "A Question of Place" was one of the finest specials NPR ever produced, he's not sure how many people actually listened to it. In a way the best cultural productions from NPR's early period became museum pieces before they even got on the air. They represented experiments in what radio could be, but there was rarely any sense that they were anything more than startling exceptions.

It had gotten to the point where stations wanted NPR to "get out of cultural programming altogether," says Jack Mitchell, who returned to the network in 1983 to oversee budget cuts in news and arts. "It was viewed as a totally ineffective sideshow."

So when NPR awoke that year to an unexpected $7.5-million deficit, it immediately turned to what it knew it could count on: news. "In the crisis mentality then, there was just one rope, and they had three drowning people. Who gets it?" says Trudeau. "The people in the arts and performance department understood that the news department was getting the rope. [Arts and performance] went from a staff of thirty or so to a staff of four. Unfortunately it was done in a series of successive waves, so it was a constant whittling down of survivors." (Accounts vary from twenty to thirty on how many staffers NPR cut from its arts and performance division.)

Mitchell says the arts division could easily have been cut to zero, but he insisted the network spend $300,000 to keep an "embryonic core to see if they could make it. The news department was furious" because the cash came out of their budget.

But at least they had a budget to beef about. By the spring of 1983, NPR's financial picture had become so bleak, many wondered if it could afford to put anything on the air.

CHAPTER SIX

The Financial Crisis

Frank Mankiewicz knew artists, politicians, and how Washington worked; but he did not know how to manage the network's finances. He left that to his lieutenants, who found themselves caught between an old system where the federal government paid for almost everything and a new system centered around money donated by private businesses and nonprofit organizations.

Public broadcasting fans have grown accustomed to hearing tag lines after their favorite shows like, "Funding for this program was provided by Xerox, the Ford Foundation, and listeners like you." But when Mankiewicz came on board in 1977, NPR basically had one funding source: the federal government. Tax dollars accounted for 90 percent of the network's budget. By the time Mankiewicz left, that figure had dropped below 50 percent and was continuing to fall. His management team had to develop a new financial plan based on multiple sources of income.

Unfortunately the president had placed his trust in people "who couldn't read a balance sheet," says Bob Edwards and many others who survived NPR's tailspin in 1983. Management could proudly talk about a doubling in audience and a quadrupling in programming hours, but no one seemed to have any idea exactly how much those gains had cost.

Too much, as Tom Warnock, the chief operating officer, had suspected and soon learned for certain. In early 1983 he went to Mankiewicz's office with the news that NPR might be $2 million in debt. The president was concerned, but considered it a manageable amount and made plans to visit a bank. A few weeks later Warnock came knocking again. Well, it seems the debt might be closer to $5 million, he said. Then a little later the figure climbed to $7 million, and finally it was guessed that it could be as much as $9 million. That represented one-third of NPR's total budget. That meant trouble.

Sloppy accounting records made it impossible to determine the full extent of the network's debt. Bills for coffee for the office were found in the long-distance telephone file. A grant for historical reporting got counted twice—once in the special projects division and again under general programming. Somewhere between 110 and 125 American Express cards had been issued, and staffers had charged something like $450,000 to $800,000 for travel and entertainment. Every department seemed to operate on ballpark figures rather than real numbers.

Tim Owens, producer for "Jazz Alive," received a 12 percent merit raise

in January 1983. Two months later NPR handed him a pink slip and canceled his show. The network increased its staff by 14 percent in 1982, then fired more than a hundred people the following year.

"Up until March, I had no reason to think we weren't on target," Mankiewicz said at the time. "Nobody had any indication of overspending."

But Warnock told the press that he had warned management about taking too many risks; the Mankiewicz vision, however, overshadowed the financial reality. "The tendency was to think, 'We can't cut back.' So there was little time spent considering the bleak scenario," Warnock said.

The Reagan administration slashed the Corporation for Public Broadcasting's funding 31 percent between 1981 and 1983, but that didn't keep Mankiewicz from asking the network's board for a 23 percent hike in the annual budget anyway. It agreed. "Sure it was a risk," Mankiewicz said, "but it was either that or cut back programs without a fight." That left the network with a $13-million gap.

Public broadcasting often complained about Congress's tight purse strings, but at least PBS and NPR could count on a set allocation. Now the radio network had to fill a hole based on income from disparate and unpredictable sources. How could it know exactly how much grant money would come in or how generous the oil corporations might feel during a recession?

It couldn't. So it took the rosiest estimates it could find and went with those. It would raise $6.3 million from grants. It would enter into some commercial ventures—sell satellite space, launch an electronic mail service and a national paging operation—and channel the profits back into NPR. It would establish a twenty-four-hour classical music service, NPR Plus, that stations could use to fill empty space in their programming. By 1987 things would be going so well that it would no longer need any federal funding. Management called the plan Project Independence.

Some of the ideas from the Mankiewicz team might have proved successful in the long run, but they completely underestimated the languorous nature of the shift from public to private funding. It couldn't just happen in a year or even two years. The transition had to be slow and conservative. At the 1984 government hearings on NPR's financial problems, Mankiewicz acknowledged that he had left "no margin for error" in all these ventures.

As it turned out, they all came up short. NPR received only half of the grant money it expected. The $700,000 it spent to start up the commercial projects bore no fruit the first year. Based on some estimates the network lost as much as $500,000 on NPR Plus because it attracted only 100 stations and needed 150 to break even. It lost another half million dollars in interest as it dipped into capital to pay its mounting bills.

Mankiewicz remained convinced that the network could escape the red ink with a bank loan, but CPB vetoed that idea. It did not want outsiders salvaging NPR. Next he tried to convince the station managers at a public radio conference in Minneapolis to make up the slack by paying double their annual dues—a backbreaking request for all the shoestring operations that make up the public radio system. They refused. "There was a feeling among member stations that NPR was a big sieve," said Kathy DeMoll, a staffer at Minnesota Public Radio at the time, "and until the sieve was plugged we weren't contributing any more money."

"It was lame," says Bill Siemering, then station manager of WHYY in Philadelphia. "How do you go on the air and say, 'We'd like your support because we've got some management problems?'"

Station managers were shocked at the unexpected news, afraid for their own survival, angry that no one had sent up any warning signals. They talked of firing Mankiewicz, but he survived two no-confidence votes and looked set to ride out the conference. Then one of his lieutenants tried to pin all the problems on a faulty new computer system that issued inaccurate financial statements. The place exploded. While the board did not call for another no-confidence vote, it was clear Mankiewicz and his staff no longer had the necessary toehold of support. The president resigned.

"I can't understand how it was possible to first see a surplus, then a $3-million problem, and then another $3-million problem," one aggravated station

NPR: Camelot In Crisis

Home Computers for the Staff, a Car
...Start of Debts & Doubts

By IRVIN MO...

THE NEW YORK TIMES, THURSDAY, JUNE 16, 1983

...as a Deficit of $6.5 Million

nationwide paging system. The auditors said that "the creation of the for-profit subsidiary was an appropriate mechanism" and should continue.

George L. Miles Jr., a Westinghouse Broadcasting executive who is on loan to Public Radio for six months to help it recover financial stability, said the network had so many overdue bills that it was developing an "aging" list to determine which delinquent bills should be paid next.

The balance sheet compiled by the auditors showed current liabi... most $9.3 million i... ...$651,000 i...

more important conclusion was that there was an absence of proper controls.

"It is not suggesting a major scandal," Mr. Jones said, referring to the auditors' finding, a position confirmed by Jerry Strong, a Coopers & Lybrand partner who worked on the audit.

In order to help eliminate the deficit, NPR has dismissed 140 employees and is seeking ... al funds.

... the acting ... said that he ... hief execu- ... 's leading ... oped they ... The foun- ... in, who ... held off ... until the

carry ... uding ... "All ... ning ... turn ... 18.5 ... ts ... fi- ... l-

---

THE NEW YORK TIMES, THURSDAY, JUNE 30, 1983

...lic Radio Stations Backing Network Aid Plan

IRVIN MOLOTSKY

...ial to The New York Times

...GTON, June 29 — The ...f the Corporation for Pub- ...sting said today that initial ... were that public radio sta- ...overwhelmingly endorsing ...keep the debt-ridden Na- ...ic Radio in operation. ...ial, Edward J. Pfister, said ...than 40 stations had already ...he plan to put up $1 million ...nity-service funds as collat- ...t the network could borrow ...d pay some of its bills. None ...ublic radio stations that re-

ceive the network's programming has rejected the plan, Mr. Pfister said.

The stations voted last week to turn over to the network $1.6 million in funds they had received from the corporation for community-service programs.

Mr. Pfister said that "creditors are knocking on the doors" at the network and that fast action was needed to stave off bankruptcy. But he said that he remained hopeful.

Ronald C. Bornstein, public radio's acting chief executive officer, said recently that bankruptcy was inevitable unless new financing were found. Reminded of Mr. Bornstein's comments, Mr. Pfister said, "We'll find a way."

The Corporation for Public Broadcasting receives a direct Federal appropriation — $137 million this year — and distributes those funds to local public radio and television stations, to National Public Radio and to the Public Broadcasting Service, which provides television programming.

However, the corporation is not permitted to provide funds to the radio network to help it reduce its deficit, which recently was estimated to ... $9.1 million. Consequently, the cor... ration has had to come up wit... roundabout plan to help the r... service.

"Public broadcasters are a... tomed to grave problems,"

Pfister said. "We'll get it resolved. I think this will be accepted by the stations. I think the service will continue."

Only one station had expressed reservations, Mr. Pfister said, and that was on technical grounds that he said could be resolved.

John Beck, who heads WNYC in ... ork City, agreed with Mr. ... ... ocal radio stations ... al over-

Dem... man... mer ... Inve... gati...

network on Ma... Mankiewicz resigned under pressure, characterized the company as "a great world of expansionism and dream, a Camelot society."

Interviews with participants in the crisis, an examination of independent audit reports, and NPR financial documents obtained by The Washington Post seem to bear out the Camelot analogy. The $9.1 million shortfall developed because, starting at the beginning of the 1983 fiscal year last Oct. 1, NPR was spending at a $30 million annual rate while income ... ...ion according to

By John McDonnell—The Washington Post
Frank Mankiewicz, ex-NPR president

NPR Eyes Severe News Cuts

New Budget Proposal Angers Staff, Stations

By Jacqueline T...

The new ... cially ...

from alarm to ange... A preliminary w... fiscal year 1984 wou... and public affairs ... $5.3 million to app... million.

"There is ... those figures," ... stein, the new a... officer of NPR.

The future sh... grams, Bornstein ... cided by the full ... don't think the fo... ...ould be ... ...ould be ... atives."

'Mor... one n... er th... whos... awar...

T... in S...

"... hav... ...two m... bara... severe... dem... unexpec... situ... ...e finan... to... nation... ...who... bac... ...ional ...we... post ... ... ex... prop... po...

NEW YORK TIMES, SATURDAY, JULY 16, 1983

...lic Radio Mounts Effort to Raise $1.8 Million by July 29

Special to The New York Times

...INGTON, July 15 — Officials ...onal Public Radio pledged ...work "round the clock" to se- ...$1.8 million needed by July 29 ... payroll and other immediate ...es, and the $9.1 million needed ...o the network alive through next

...on to reviving the negotia- ...

tors. The network estimates that by the end of the fiscal year, on Sept. 1, it will have a debt of $9.1 million.

Although the exact terms of the proposed loan are not public, officials said that an agreement hinges on the pledge of at least 200 of the network's 281 stations to repay the loan out of their Federal grants if public radio defaults.

The decision on the loan was delayed, according to a spokesman for Public Broadcast- ... ...t number of

two of public radio's most popular shows — will be broadcast by participating stations. Money raised by the effort will first be applied by the individual stations to their shares of $1.6 million that member stations had pledged to the network in May. All additional funds will go directly to

... or of WNYC in ... largest mem- ... ns, yesterday sent a tele- ... to Bornstein expressing his outrage.

"It said this is a critical issue for us and we will carry on the debat... any way we can." s... opinio...

national programming budget.

"I guess if we don't get the money by July 29, the August fund-raiser will be irrelevant," said a network staff member. "But we have to look toward the future. We can't sit at our desks and say 'Oh, well, in two weeks we'll go bust.'"

... emporary chie... ...esigned NPR, Mankiewicz fo... ...memos to the staff on contacts ...the press, the board member. ...NPR and the Corporation for Pu... Broadcasting, the federal age... that assists in funding NPR. T... memos instructed that ... contacts b...

NPR Gets Warning

Standoff Jeopardizes Federal Payment

By Jacqueline Trescott

The Corporation for Pu[blic] Broadcasting not only stood f[irm] yesterday on its conditions for a life-saving loan to National Public Ra[dio] ... that it may ...

---

block the $1 mil[lion] ... ment it is schedul[ed] send to NPR on [...]

"NPR is a [...] CPB presiden[t ...] He told repo[rters ...] tinue to i[...] title to [...] equipm[ent ...] $9.1 [...] trus[t ...] li[...]

FRANK J. PRIAL

Frank Mankiewicz, president of National Public Radio, resigned as chief operating officer yesterday.

The announcement was made at the annual Minneapolis Public Radio Conference in Minneapolis, where it was learned that the 13-year-old radio network was experiencing unexpectedly serious financial problems.

Broadcasters familiar with the network's financial situation said the board had been surprised to discover that a budget deficit estimated only a month ago at about $2.8 million was actually closer to $5.8 million.

"If it's going to meet their payroll," one public broadcasting executive said.

Last week, Mr. Mankiewicz unveiled a plan to close the $2.8 million gap by having the 276 member stations pay a fee for each program they took from the network. The stations pay annual dues that entitle [them to] any or all of network's va[...]

[...]icz Leaving Public Radio

THE NEW YORK T[IMES]

gram offerings. The board was expected to vote late yesterday or today on whether to initiate the fee proposal or to cut programming.

Mr. Mankiewicz, who joined the network in 1977, instituted a variety of new programming and more than doubled the network's audience. He said he would stay on as president while a new chief operating officer would be involved in financial and legislative relations until he left the organization.

"I said two years ago that we ought to have a separate operating officer," Mr. Mankiewicz said in a telephone interview.

He later added: "It [...] self-serving to say [...] anyway, but I [...] years in a f[...] enough [...]

officer would have "full responsibil[ity] for day-to-day operational and managerial decisions and will report directly to the board."

The conference is, in effect, the annual meeting of National Public Radio's board of directors.

In addition to the proposal on fees, the board was to consider a proposal to permit the network to seek funds through its member stations. Until now, it has relied on the annual dues of the member stations [...] the Corpor[ation ...]

[...] Fate of Public Radio May Be Decided Today

NATIONAL PUBLIC RADIO

[Con]tinued From Page A1

[...] of Michigan, who is chair[man of the] House Energy and Com[merce] committee on Oversight and [investigati]ons, has ordered an investi[gation of] the General Accounting Of[fice to det]ermine responsibility for the [...] results are due in Septem[ber ...] Dingell has prom[ised ...]

Network [...]

[...] budget for [...] the news [...] et from [...]

[...] roblems have [...] ngress and else[where ...]

June of last year has been distributing programs to member stations that pay about $850 a year in membership fees. The best-known of these programs is "Prairie Home Companion," a jovial weekly variety show hosted by Garrison Keillor.

While last winter, member public stations carried about half of the 40 hours of programs offered each week [...] Public Radio, today they [...]

NPR Gets $500,000 Interest-Free Loan

By Jacqueline Trescott

After fears mounted that National Public Radio would be unable to meet tomorrow's payroll, the Corporation for Public B[roadcasting pro]vided a [...] y pro[gram ...] 00,000 [...] cash[...]

Lawyers for NPR and CPB, which aids in funding public broadcasting, along with CPB president Ed[ward Pfister, met for more than four hours in Wash[ington working out the details of the loan. Pfister] could not be reached for comment.

The network's deficit, which Mankiewicz originally estimated at $2.8 million, is now put at $5.8 million, [...] estimate that might be further revised after an [...] both NPR and the General Ac[counting ...] change the pro[gramming of the] network.

[...] artments, the [...] 1984 budget [...] management [...] -case scenario, [...] n has said he [...] d performance [...] 0. In the first [...] lost "The Sun[day Show" and] Jazz Alive." The [...] news portions of [...] ted to the largest [...] c affairs. "The last [...] n is on-air produc[tion ...]

NPR, From C1

[...]tion,' I only gave them [...]ine. I felt it was the prop[er thing to] do," said Fitzmaurice, [...]ams have won numerous [...]

[...]s unit will close its bureau [in New York] City.

"[...]'t reduce your staff without [a]ffect the quality," said Bar[rett Hamilto]n, the outgoing vice presi[dent for new]ws and information. "The [situation is] very fluid, and if you talk [next] week I bet they will all be [back] if we could have $110,000, [to s]ave some jobs."

[...]ings take effect in 20 days [and there is] a 40-day period for the re[...]

[...] who is moving to NBC, will [be replac]ed by Robert Siegel, currently [an] editor based in London, who [beca]me the acting director of news [infor]mation on June 2.

[Earlie]r this week the 17-member [bo]ard approved a $17.65 million [budget] for fiscal 1984, down from [$xx mi]llion for fiscal 1983. NPR of[ficials] have steadily raised their esti[mate of] the deficit from $2.8 million [...]

NPR Fires 84; News Division Loses 17

The firings came at a time when the management has received offers of financial assistance from the staff, some of the member stations, and some businesses and foundations.

In the past three weeks, said Jane Couch, vice president for development, three foundations that had not granted money to NPR previously have given a total of $200,000. "I can't give you the foundation names," said Couch, adding that "in the last three days we have [rec]eived $4,974 in checks from 130 [...]

Earlier this week management-level employes of the news department offered to take a 10 percent wage cut for the remainder of fiscal 1983 and in 1984 in order to save positions.

"Bornstein, in effect, said, 'We are taking a look at that,' " said Washington bureau chief John McChesney.

Jack Taub, the president of a tel[e]communications firm that formed[a] joint venture with NPR last year [to] send computerized data through [the] NPR satellite, offered to lend or [guar]antee a $1 million loan to Mank[iewicz] a few months ago. The project [re]ceived approval from the [Federal] Communications Commission [and] awaits registration approval [from the] Securities and Exchange C[ommission.] Taub said his offer was st[ill open. "I] have not talked directly [with new] management, but I am [not going to] back away from my wor[d ...]

Though some emplo[yes ...] that the managemen[t ...] standing still on th[...] Jane Couch said, "[...] Bornstein's full co[operation. He] had funders in he[re ...] himself available [...] tice."

The commit[tee ...] board to stud[y ...]

NPR: The Dream Failed

Missing the Mark With Bid For Financial Independence

Second of Two Articles

By Phil McCombs and Jacqueline Trescott

Jane A. Couch, a dynamic [...] 15 years' experien[ce ...] fundraiser [...]

manager told a reporter. "I can't understand why there weren't whistles blowing and flags waving."

Well, they began blowing and waving after the conference. The news department lost twenty people, including seven reporters. The arts department lost 79 percent of its budget and all but seven of its staffers. Newspaper headlines chronicled the disaster: "NPR Fires 84," "National Public Radio's Saddest Story Is Its Own," "NPR: The Dream Failed," "On the NPR Roller Coaster."

"On the next payday, we didn't know if that was going to be the last one," says Bob Edwards. "We were borrowing paper from CBS across the street."

"At some point someone told us that we only had two days left, so collect your personal belongings," Jay Kernis recalls. "We were told they would be selling the tape machines.

"We came within one day of closing. I felt betrayed. Betrayed is the only word. How could they do this to us? This place is so remarkable, so sacred."

Each hour became a marathon as Kernis and his "Morning Edition" staff struggled to produce a program with rapidly diminishing resources. "My staff won't last till October," he told a *Washington Post* reporter in 1983. "They're so overworked. We've lost three producer positions, and the pressure is tremendous. Our people are sick more often and stay out longer, and a lot of them have been asking me for job references."

Steve Reiner, then executive producer of "All Things Considered," made similar remarks: "There's a shortage of material because there's no money. Freelancers tend not to want to work for us because they still haven't got paid for work done."

Susan Stamberg recalls a similarly bleak scene: "It was devastating to come to work and all the faces would be gone. And there were days when we weren't sure if we were going to get into the building because the rent wasn't paid. That's how bad it was."

But the largest gash opened in the network's arts and performance division. "What NPR was, is no longer—and that is the vision that it had for cultural programming," Ken Myers, editor of the defunct "Sunday Show," told reporters. "What is upsetting is that it's cutting back all but the two programs ['Morning Edition' and 'All Things Considered'] that are most like other things being provided elsewhere in other media. The programs being canceled are the ones that were doing something unique. There's nothing like 'Jazz Alive' anywhere else in the country."

At least the remaining "ATC" staffers had a sense of humor. "You know what we did in the middle of it?" laughs Stamberg. "Noah and I walked over with our microphones—it was summer—and sat in Dupont Circle [in the heart of downtown Washington] and just talked to each other on tape about a summer afternoon. Actually it turned out to be a very charming piece.

"Then a couple weeks later we went up on the roof and did a helicopter traffic report. I had wanted to do that for years. 'There is no helicopter traffic in the air at this moment,' I said."

70

Adams may have managed a few laughs because he felt far less anxious about the possible demise of the network than most of his colleagues. "It wouldn't have bothered me a whole lot if NPR had closed down," he says. "I think that public radio is an important thing, and by '83 there had been more than ten years of public radio. Someone else would have come along. There would have been other producers."

Someone did come along, albeit unwillingly: the Corporation for Public Broadcasting. CPB established a tense working relationship with Ronald Bornstein, who left his job as director of the University of Wisconsin's telecommunications division to become NPR's acting president. Bornstein supervised a cleanup crew that included George Miles, a financial advisor on loan from the Westinghouse Corporation; and a cadre of lawyers and accountants from some of the biggest firms in Washington. They sorted through files, tracked down unpaid bills, and cleared away some cobwebs.

But all the scrubbing didn't take away the fact that the network needed money. Immediately. Member stations continued to whine about fund raising for NPR, because they feared it would detract from their own local efforts. Somehow they missed the point that they wouldn't have much of a local show if they didn't save their primary program producer. Desperate, NPR took the avenue of last resort and used "All Things Considered" to appeal to listeners directly. For a

Saving NPR from financial ruin wasn't easy. Ronald Bornstein (far left) was called in from Wisconsin to be acting president. Tim Wirth (center) swung his congressional clout to get relief from CPB, and Sharon Rockefeller (left) at CPB, though committed to public broadcasting, constantly tussled with Frank Mankiewicz over what was needed.

week Stamberg and Adams included a fund-raising segment, "The Drive to Survive," in their ninety-minute newscast—the first and only time the network has ever solicited on the air.

"There were two versions," recalls Bill Siemering, who pushed for the idea as a member of NPR's board. "Some stations didn't want any of this on the air, so they took the 'ATC' without the 'Drive to Survive.' Only a third of the stations participated in it. A rather rag-tag group. It was their own provincialism that prevented them from doing it.

"It was the easiest fund-raiser I've ever done in my life. Just give the phone number and the people went crazy. The money just rolled in."

They netted $2,250,000 in just three days. Mankiewicz insists that the entire problem could have been solved if all the stations had gotten involved. "Hell," he said at the time, "we're only talking about a few million dollars. The United States government is going to have a deficit of $250 billion, and their president's not resigning."

Siemering agrees with Mankiewicz's assessment. "The debt would have been history if everyone had done it."

But it wasn't history. So NPR and CPB began a long battle over the terms for a loan to the network. The corporation wanted to scrutinize every financial decision, which NPR saw as an attempt to control content. It wanted the title to

73

the network's satellite transmission equipment as collateral. Ronald Bornstein fought the restrictions. Nasty letters went back and forth, and the two sides wound up in a stalemate.

"We were within hours of going off the air," recalls Cokie Roberts. "We were saved in the end by the U.S. Congress. The chairman of the Subcommittee on Telecommunications, Rep. Tim Wirth, got involved in all of it. He sent his staff to CPB and said, 'Fix it.' That's what it required, someone saying that it's not up to you guys. It had become a macho shoot-out. They needed someone from the outside to come in and say, 'We don't care how big you are, this is a national institution and Congress cares about it and the country cares about it—so fix it.'"

The two sides sweated in a room for more than twelve hours before settling on a plan. NPR finally agreed to release its satellite equipment to a three-person trustee group—not CPB. In return the network received a $9.1-million line of credit as part of a three-year loan.

Through it all NPR's news staff tracked their own story. News director Barbara Cohen chose Scott Simon, then a Chicago bureau chief, for the beat, because she felt he would have a more objective perspective than someone caught in the quicksand at the Washington headquarters. Simon had spent the previous year covering the war in El Salvador. He found NPR's story equally difficult "because virtually everyone you speak with thinks he knows the answers," he told *The New York Times*.

> NPR was bankrupt. Period. Frank had never run a big organization before. The problem was that he didn't see that it was a problem.
> — *Sharon Rockefeller, former CPB board chair*

"These are the very worst times in the thirteen-year history of National Public Radio," he announced to "Morning Edition" listeners on May 17, 1983, "and they are occurring in a time, ironically, when the network's audience has never been larger, its programming more extensive, or its reputation for excellence greater."

He interviewed shattered staffers like Jay Kernis, who told Simon, "Every day is like a month, because half your brain is thinking, 'It's gonna end. What if I have to fire another staff member?' It's always there. It's lousy."

Simon even convinced Mankiewicz to come on the air, then pulled no punches. "What happened, of course, is that we underestimated the length and depth of the recession," the ex-president explained.

"See, to some people," retorted Simon, "the question arises, how could someone who not only listens to the two daily news programs that National Public Radio does, but also . . . has a hand in them, be surprised by that?"

A shadow crossed Mankiewicz's voice as he paused, then replied, "There you have a failure of management for which I'm not only willing to take the blame, but already have. [He resigned.] We simply lacked either the people or the tools to track it."

Their exchanges shifted from tense to tragic as Simon pointed out that Mankiewicz's financial stumble had destroyed much of the vision the former president had worked so hard to realize. "The reductions which might now be made and the programs that could be jeopardized are exactly those advances in news and entertainment to which Frank Mankiewicz was most devoted," the reporter said. "For many of the employees of National Public Radio, there's an intimate kind of anger in this.

"There are people in this building who have worked for you, who love you, truly," he continued. "And yet, some of those people believe that they did their job and put out the best programming possible and that you and other managers failed in their jobs, and now they're going to have to pay the price."

"I feel a great deal of that pain," replied Mankiewicz darkly, "and I think it's largely true. But there are other sides to it."

It remains unclear exactly what the "other sides" were. Today when asked about the situation in 1983, Mankiewicz says, "I think what really happened was I lost a fight. I might have lost anyway. The financial problems accelerated it, but they were not serious. [CPB board chair] Sharon Rockefeller was trying to get me out. We could have borrowed the money with no problem."

He says that he and Rockefeller had long fights about getting more funding from the federal government. Mankiewicz believed the bulk of public broadcasting's budget should come from somewhere else because too many key social programs, like Head Start and Aid for Dependent Children, had to fight for the same small pie. "I was seriously thinking of taking radio out of CPB," he says. Instead, NPR's board muscled Mankiewicz out of his job.

"That's absolutely untrue," says Rockefeller, now president of Washington, D.C.'s public broadcasting station, WETA. "There was no politics involved whatsoever. Frank was successful in building NPR, but no one has accused him of being a businessman." Mankiewicz kept the network's bleak financial picture from CPB, which only aggravated the situation, she adds. She heard reports of a $3-million debt, then $6 million, but no solid figures or records. "We had no

Scott Simon and NPR both survived the network's financial crisis. At the time, Simon said, "These are the very worst times in the . . . history of National Public Radio, . . . ironically when its . . . audience has never been larger, its programming more extensive, or its reputation for excellence greater."

choice. We had to get involved before $6 million ballooned into $9 million. NPR was bankrupt. Period. Frank had never run a big organization before. The problem was that he didn't see that it was a problem."

Rockefeller does acknowledge that she and Mankiewicz had some tough battles over funding before 1983. In particular, she recalls the time the NPR president went over CPB's head directly to Congress to win a guaranteed 25 percent of the corporation's annual budget for the radio network instead of the customary 10 to 15 percent. "There's a 10-to-1 cost ratio between television and radio," she says, "but he insisted on 25 percent anyway. He never hears the other side of the story."

Whatever the political reality, evidence presented at the congressional hearings in 1983 and 1984 showed all too clearly that NPR's management had handled its finances irresponsibly. Mankiewicz offered some convincing counterpoints on many of the allegations, but he left too many destructive pieces of evidence dangling.

After listening to testimony from Ronald Bornstein and other members of the NPR cleanup crew, Congressman Steny Hoyer concluded: "Essentially, management did not know how much it had in the checkbook." That oversight lay at the root of Tornado '83.

NPR lived hand-to-mouth for the next eighteen months, says Doug Bennet, who joined the network in 1983 as president. "I had to cut the budget eight times during that period, because something would be discovered that required a tuck. There were no books—literally. Every time there was a staff meeting everyone was edgy, skeptical, cynical."

But at least most of the dirty work had been done by the time Bennet arrived. He didn't have to fire anyone. He spent most of his time reassuring people. "Yes, the debt was being paid back. Yes, the network was still here." By 1985 NPR had paid back the $7 million it owed and actually showed a $250,000 surplus. "We'd turned the corner," he says.

And ran smack into CPB—again. The two sides couldn't agree on how to spend some extra money Congress had allocated. They bickered until CPB turned its back and created a Radio Fund for the money without telling NPR's management. Anyone could apply for the cash—not just the network.

"That was a fundamental sea change," says current Radio Fund director Rick Madden. "One hundred percent of our dollars had been going to NPR. Now some money was available competitively."

NPR first heard of the new deal at the station managers' conference in San Francisco. "They were furious," says Madden. "They felt they could no longer count on CPB as a reliable partner. By February of that year NPR announced its business plan. Their proposal was—'We want CPB to give *all* the money to the stations, and the stations will decide what programming they want.'"

That meant no more CPB as political middleman and no more monopoly for NPR. Now the stations sat in the driver seat. Instead of getting an entire NPR package for a fee, they could choose what they wanted and pay for programs individually. If they had a project idea of their own, they could apply to the Radio Fund for a grant rather than try to sell the idea to NPR. The "unbundling" process took years to implement—in many ways it's still ongoing—but it ended what Bennet describes as a "poisoned relationship on all sides."

It also created a market-driven mentality that fundamentally altered the mission of NPR. "Sometime around '84 or '85 we declared that building an audience was an important goal for the system," says Bennet. "It had been a debatable point before that."

Specialized programs and experimental programs could no longer ride on the coattails of a larger package of more established shows. If the stations felt something wouldn't draw an audience in their area, they just didn't buy it.

The trade-off, of course, is that NPR no longer has to deal with a fickle Congress or a politicized CPB. The network gets less than 1 percent of its budget from the corporation; the rest comes from stations' fees, foundations, private companies, and "listeners like you." Indirectly about 15 percent of NPR's budget comes from tax dollars, because the stations themselves use some federal funds to pay the network.

The debate over funding for public broadcasting continues in the 1990s, indicating that changes in NPR's financial structure may all be for the best. Congress has never been a reliable partner. It took years for it to agree on a long-range funding plan for public radio and TV, and just as the three-year cycle kicked in, Republicans in the White House—especially during the Reagan administration—began lobbying for cuts in the proposed budget. This left public broadcasting in a financial no-man's-land: some federal funding but never enough.

Throughout the 1983 and 1984 hearings on the radio network's debt, representatives rightly accused Mankiewicz of "gross mismanagement" that led to alleged credit card abuse, diversion of withholding taxes, personal use of corporate property, provision of interest-free loans for employees, and other inexcusable actions. Not surprisingly, however, they did not acknowledge their own contri-

Doug Bennet (above) and Frank Mankiewicz (below). Two presidents, two different styles, but with something important in common: a devotion to NPR and a determination to preserve its preeminent place in American broadcast journalism.

bution to NPR's financial mess and certainly did not like being accused of fiscal irresponsibility in general.

When the dethroned NPR president gamely pointed out at the 1984 hearing "that the federal deficit for the government of the United States has increased by more than the total amount of the NPR deficit just since I began my testimony," committee chairman John Dingell retaliated with a harsh reprimand.

"I would warn you that that kind of discussion probably triggers a severe attack on the budget of NPR and CPB," he said. "That may not be a matter of concern to you, sir, but it is to me."

"I intended it as an aside," Mankiewicz replied, knowing full well that the Congress had hardly played a "side" role in the very problems that stalled and nearly killed his vision for NPR.

Indeed, despite the horrible situation Mankiewicz's management team left behind, almost no one who worked there then has anything ill to say of the former president now. Nina Totenberg thinks he was a scapegoat. Bob Edwards refuses to forget that the ex-president fathered "Morning Edition." Cokie Roberts credits him for "making NPR a major news operation, for proving it was not college radio." Former "Talk of the Nation" host John Hockenberry bluntly states: "This place hasn't had a mission since Frank Mankiewicz left." Hockenberry himself left in the summer of 1992 to work with ABC.

Even Jay Kernis, who felt downright "betrayed" at the time, credits Mankiewicz for taking the blame and standing behind his faulty lieutenants. "He put public radio on the map," he says. "He had a true vision. He told us to grow up. He put us in the big time. He fought the White House when it wanted to influence content. He fought a lot of big battles for us. I can't say that he should have looked at the books. That's what his VPs should have been doing. Of course, all of this may be very revisionist of me," he adds.

Compared with newspaper accounts from 1983, most of these comments reflect a kinder, gentler interpretation of events. Former staffers have come to terms with the pain they suffered because, after all, the network did survive and has never entered the shadows of anonymity again. But Mankiewicz's achievements as a public relations wizard will always be balanced against the financial failures of his reign at NPR. Perhaps the tragic flaw lay in his belief that he could run the network like a political campaign rather than a business.

Today Mankiewicz is more apt to point to political in-fighting as the cause of his undoing, but in 1983 he told a magazine reporter that he and his staff had taken a gamble and lost. "We guessed wrong," he said. "Like Bogart said in *Casablanca*, 'I was misinformed.'"

CHAPTER SEVEN

Tuning In

The people who really saved NPR in 1983 had nothing to do with all the infighting, politics, overworked staffers, and tearful goodbyes. They simply tuned in while taking a shower, milking their cows, or driving from work. They listened to what seemed like the death throes of *their* radio network and began sending unsolicited checks and letters like flowers to a funeral. Five dollars. Ten dollars. An apology for not sending more. "Life without NPR—particularly 'All Things Considered'—is unthinkable," wrote one Silver Spring, Maryland, couple. "We wish we could make a handsomer contribution."

NPR fans easily could have gotten their news and entertainment from somewhere else: Peter Jennings, Tom Brokaw, Dan Rather, *The New York Times,* the local paper, a favorite sit-com, a local country music station. In a multimedia society, what could one radio network possibly mean? A great deal, especially for the person driving down a two-lane road in a place like Maine, Iowa, or West Virginia.

Only a small percentage of the 250 million people who live in this country actually read *The New York Times* or any other major metropolitan newspaper. Print news for most Americans comes down to whatever the lone local paper decides it wants to write about: the county fair, the man who plowed through widow Johnson's picket fence. Network television has a wider reach, but it doesn't travel like radio—either on the road, in the field, or in the mind.

"I find when I do television," says Susan Stamberg, "people say, 'I *saw* you on television.' When I do radio they say, 'I *heard* you on radio.' The content gets through."

When farmers or backroad travelers flick to the public station at the low end of their radio dial, they can hear of orphans dying in Bosnia, of Clinton on the campaign trail, of crude jokes about pubic hairs on Anita Hill's Coke. NPR gives them sounds from a wider world that reflect and provide a context for their own humanity.

"In small communities, where you're not inundated with other information, NPR is still really prized," says Bill Siemering, who spent a large portion of his public radio career at stations in Minnesota and Wisconsin.

Fifty thousand listeners tune in each week to programs on public station KUNI in Cedar Falls, Iowa. They hear soul music on "BluesStage" and Irish ballads on "Thistle and Shamrock." They catch Bob Edwards at 5 a.m. before heading to the barn or Noah Adams on "All Things Considered" on their car

NORTON UNITED METHODIST CHUR[CH]

August 9,

[...]wn Road
[...]o 44203

Mr. Scott Simon
National Public Radio
Washington, D. C.

Dear Mr. Simon:

Every Saturday morning, as I make my morning coffee
begin the arduous task of final sermon preparation, I t[urn]
on WKSU and listen to Weekend Edition. You have become
good friend who has brought joy and laughter, tears an[d]
compassion into my day at a time when I need it most.

I was especially moved by the report on Maryville
was broadcast yesterday, August 8, 1987. However, the[...]
[...] interviews which I have apprecia[ted]

[...]
A[...]
N[...]al Public Radio
Washington, DC 20[05]6

Dear Staff of All Things Considered:

Since 1978 I have been listening almost daily to All Th[ings]
Considered and in all these years I have never written to yo[u]
However I have found Andrei Codrescue's reports of his retur[n to]
Roumania so rivetting, so moving-- tears actually came to my [eyes]
while listening to him-- that I am prompted to break my silen[ce]
of twelve years and say that if there is a Pulitzer Prize for
broadcasting he should receive it.

I am a painter. How often in these past twelve years I ha[ve]
sat painting while listening to you. How many dozens and dozen[s]
of paintings I have made inspired by your program. [...]
not own a television my sou[...]

[...]
NPR
Washington, D.C. 2003[...]

Dear Mr. Simon:

I don't often writ[e]
or television; how[...]
special I feel con[...]
I try never to miss[...]
noon and two on C[...]

your interviewing [...]
abrasive, and your [...]
uncanny in its ab[...]

Dear Scott,
    Just a belat[ed]
of thanks [...]
my Saturd[...]
style.
    Some[...]
reports ar[...]
almost pa[...]
in the [...]
[...]few men[...]
the gu[...]

feel
i|9|[...]
NP[R]
WA[...]

DE[...]
i[...]
SIN[...]
BE[...]
BER[...]
IS TH[...]
THA[...]
S[...]
80 TALK[...]
NEAR[...]
REGA[...]

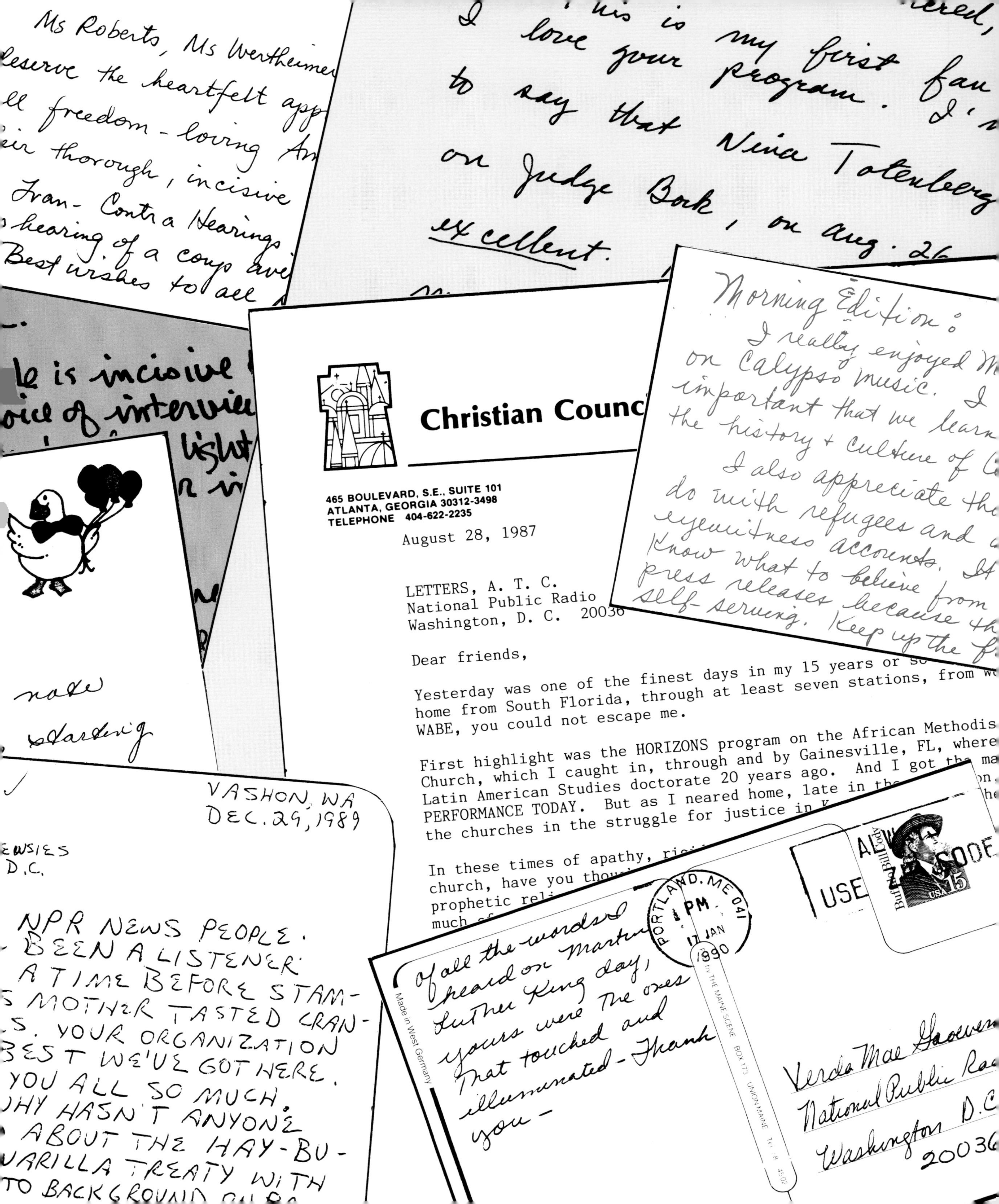

Ms Roberts, Ms Wertheimer
deserve the heartfelt app
all freedom-loving Am
their thorough, incisive
Iran-Contra Hearings
hearing of a coup ave
Best wishes to all

I ... this is my first fan
love your program. I'm
to say that Nina Totenberg
on Judge Bork, on Aug. 26
excellent.

le is incisive
oice of interview
light

note
starting

Christian Counc

465 BOULEVARD, S.E., SUITE 101
ATLANTA, GEORGIA 30312-3498
TELEPHONE 404-622-2235

August 28, 1987

LETTERS, A. T. C.
National Public Radio
Washington, D. C. 20036

Dear friends,

Yesterday was one of the finest days in my 15 years or so ... home from South Florida, through at least seven stations, from w... WABE, you could not escape me.

First highlight was the HORIZONS program on the African Methodis... Church, which I caught in, through and by Gainesville, FL, where... Latin American Studies doctorate 20 years ago. And I got the ma... PERFORMANCE TODAY. But as I neared home, late in the ... the churches in the struggle for justice in K...

In these times of apathy, ... church, have you thou... prophetic rel... much ...

Morning Edition:
I really enjoyed M...
on Calypso music. I ...
important that we learn
the history + culture of ...
I also appreciate the ...
do with refugees and ...
eyewitness accounts. It ...
know what to believe from ...
press releases because th...
self-serving. Keep up the f...

VASHON, WA
DEC. 29, 1989

...EWSIES
D.C.

NPR NEWS PEOPLE.
BEEN A LISTENER
A TIME BEFORE STAM-
MOTHER TASTED CRAN-
S. YOUR ORGANIZATION
BEST WE'VE GOT HERE.
YOU ALL SO MUCH.
WHY HASN'T ANYONE
ABOUT THE HAY-BU-
NARILLA TREATY WITH
TO BACKGROUND ...

Of all the words I
heard on Martin
Luther King day,
yours were the ones
that touched and
illuminated - Thank
you -

Made in West Germany

PORTLAND, ME 041
PM
17 JAN
1990

USE ... ZIP CODE

Buffalo Bill Cody
USA 15

THE MAINE SCENE BOX 173 UNION MAINE

Verda Mae Grosvenor
National Public Rad...
Washington D.C.
20036

"The voices and personalities on National Public Radio constitute a sort of family for me; without them I would feel bereft," wrote one listener. Scott Simon (above) and Susan Stamberg (opposite) are the adopted siblings of millions of Americans.

radios if they're commuting home from the city after work. "We have a really mixed audience," says KUNI program director Carl Jenkins. "We get these stories about farmers who are driving air-conditioned tractors and listening to Beethoven. There's probably some truth to that.

"NPR does very well in the Midwest. My guess is that in raw numbers it does better in major metropolitan areas, but I think a larger percentage of the people here listen."

Cedar Falls certainly can't match the huge audience NPR draws in a place like New York City. Scott Borden, program director at WNYC-FM, estimates that 430,000 fans tune in each week to hear "Morning Edition," "All Things Considered," "Afropop Worldwide," and other programs. But offering "Afropop" in New York isn't quite the same as offering it in Iowa. "Public stations in rural areas tend to be the only game in town," says Borden, "so they actually have to be more careful. We can focus on highly specialized areas in the arts—like a specific genre of classical music—but you can't do that in a rural market where you're the only classical station. So WNYC actually has more freedom, though we certainly have to work harder to stay ahead of all the competition."

NPR plays to a much larger audience in places like Philadelphia, Chicago, and Boston; but big does not necessarily translate into significant. It's in the less populated areas of America that the network most completely fulfills its role as a public service. It plugs programming gaps in the heartland that a resident of the Bronx could never imagine existing on his radio.

Listeners in all areas of America continue to tune in to their radios at record rates, despite repeated accounts that the medium could never survive the onslaught of television. Radio's resilience stands as a tribute to the enduring allure of a human voice appealing to a curious ear. It draws on an oral tradition of storytelling that existed before pictures, before print. No matter what tricks radio plays with sound, it must always come back to "a single voice involved in communication," says Stamberg. This simplicity fosters an intimacy with listeners that no other form of media can match, which helps explain why NPR fans tend to take everything the network does personally.

"I wonder if you realize how much the programs on WFPL mean to me and to many others," one woman wrote to the public station in Bob Edwards's hometown of Louisville, Kentucky. "Since I cannot read a newspaper I rely largely on your station for current events, as well as for commentators' opinions on those events. I have breakfast with 'Morning Edition,' and I have dinner with 'All Things Considered.' The voices and personalities on National Public Radio constitute a sort of family for me; without them I would feel bereft."

Another listener in Tacoma, Washington, tells of waking up to the "beautiful melody" of a button on "Morning Edition." "It filled me with endorphins," he exclaims. "I got up and played it by ear on my Baldwin grand."

Of course, not all letters are quite so effusive. "Morning Edition" director Barry Gordemer keeps a postcard over his desk from a listener who also took NPR's music selection personally: "Damn! Who is choosing the so-called buttons for all your programs now? I am turning the whole program off—such ugly sounds."

Even when NPR came within pennies of going off the air in 1983, it received some harsh mail. "All in all I am delighted with the prospect of the demise of NPR," one listener wrote, "given what a perverse version of world events it presents and how it stifles the growth of legitimate local news organizations."

The network rarely gets such pointed criticism, particularly through the mail. Today's touch-tone generation is much more apt to phone in their opinions. NPR has made that easy with its use of 800 numbers during major events like the Gulf War. Callers left messages on a voice "mailbox," then "Morning Edition" and "All Things Considered" aired selected responses.

The audio letters often caught the tone and intensity of NPR's audience better than the print letters read by the hosts, because they captured quivers of anger, satirical notes, and quirky diction. During one "Morning Edition" program a woman chastised NPR for concluding a story on the death of a ten-year-old Iraqi boy with a reminder that the Iraqi government only released material it wished to air. "Does this somehow ameliorate the death of a child?" she asked in a voice full of tearful breaks. "Where's our humanity?"

Another wartime voice-mail item broadcast on "All Things Considered" captured the cynical side of NPR listeners: "You got so much mileage out of Neal Conan getting hijacked," chided one man after the NPR reporter had been snagged and later released by the Iraqi Republican Guard, "that I wonder if you paid the hijackers. You don't have to repeat the story every fifteen minutes, but I am glad he's home now."

Although the news programs do get more than

a thousand written requests a month for tapes and transcripts, it's specific stars, not stories, that generate the most personal letters and phone calls. Former "Weekend Edition" host Scott Simon—a.k.a. "Mr. Sensitivity"—pulled in the most marriage proposals before his departure for NBC in the summer of 1992.

"You're such a delight," wrote one infatuated listener from New York City. "My crush on you only increases with the years." Another scorned fan scolded him for not answering her letters: "Did you get my fortieth birthday card? Or are you just too famous to answer my mail?"

A man from Albion, Missouri, seemed less taken by Simon's charms: "A while back you had Scott somebody touring Alaska or taking river trips someplace in the U.S. He sounded like he was brain dead."

When she hosted regularly, Susan Stamberg elicited an equally personal response from listeners: "Alas, this clipping is all I know about Susan's leaving 'All Things Considered,'" wrote one distraught Charlottesville, Virginia, fan, who enclosed a copy of a small announcement from her local paper. "I am *very* unhappy about it and must have more information."

But then another listener made a point of letting the host know that he suffered no such pangs of loss: "Ms. Stamberg's announcing leaves much to be desired. There is always a hint of a smile in her voice and a chuckle underneath every word, even when reporting on the evisceration of a young peasant girl in El Salvador."

Noah Adams (below), like Bob Edwards a native of Kentucky, is an accomplished writer as well as a much-praised host and broadcaster.

In general fans want pictures of Bob Edwards, breakfast with Noah Adams. They want to know why Cokie Roberts sounds tired or whether Congress has pressured Nina Totenberg for breaking the Anita Hill story.

The most poignant letters about general NPR programming seem to come from people on the move. One Canadian couple who traveled from Fort Myers, Florida, to Toronto credited the network with salvaging their road trip. They spent long hours alone with American radio programming. NPR's evening concerts saved them from the cacophony of commercial sounds. Another note arrived from Hong Kong on Hilton Hotel stationery: "This is my first fan letter ever," it said. "I'm writing because I'm having a major NPR withdrawal here in Hong Kong, where I've been transferred."

And still another from Turkey: "I'm the lady who called collect from a little convenience store to pledge $60 to your fund drive early last April. . . . Well, I may be your only nonlistening 'listener' for reasons beyond my control. I haven't figured out

84

how to pick up FM radio from Kansas on a short-wave system in Ankara, Turkey, where I currently live and work."

The intimate tone of so many of these letters distinguishes them from the sort received by daily newspapers or television stations. A man wants NPR to know he has a Baldwin grand piano. A woman not only tells them that she's moved, but, indirectly, she also expects them to care.

"People name cats and dogs and children after us," says Cokie Roberts.

Susan Stamberg first forged this uniquely personal connection with NPR's audience by dropping the impersonal approach to newscasting and taking on a more neighborly tone as host of "ATC" during the 1970s. Fans sent her flowers or soup if she sounded sick or sad. "There was a level of care there," she says, but she senses that it may be slipping away. As a primary news source for news-starved towns, NPR can no longer afford to be quite so "embracing. It's a much smoother, slicker enterprise, and it's a much more professional endeavor. Those soft spots I talked about are pretty much gone.

Nina Totenberg, now most often associated with the Anita Hill-Clarence Thomas story, has had a long career of being ahead of her competition around the Supreme Court.

"It is sad." She pauses before adding, almost in a whisper, "I do think they [the current 'ATC' staff] take themselves too seriously. Though it *is* a serious enterprise. It's become people's first source of information," which represents quite a shift from the days when listeners tuned in to get more offbeat takes on mainstream stories or just stories that no other form of media would consider covering, like Life Savers sparking in the dark.

Stamberg sustained her intimate approach to the news even as NPR's audience grew into the millions, because in her mind she was always talking to one person—her husband.

"It's something I learned from Alistair Cooke early on. He said you can never think of *listeners*—you can only think of one. If I had to think that I had 10 million people listening to me, I'd get lockjaw. It influences the way I speak. I always feel that it's one person—mostly my husband—especially when I started. Now whenever I sit for Bob [Edwards], I call my husband and tell him to listen in. He's a wonderful, intelligent, interactive listener."

Even though Stamberg never wanted to picture all ears on her, her voice still reached into people's daily lives. Cokie Roberts recalls that one farmer wrote to say that his cows stopped milking when Stamberg left NPR to write a book. "They had gotten so used to her voice in the shed," Roberts says with a laugh. "It took him a while to figure that one out."

Many staffers at NPR don't want to soothe cows anymore. They want the

85

network to break from the "embracing" tones of the past and move into the hardcore news style of the 1990s. It's just all part of a major news organization coming of age, they say.

"Maybe there was a bit too much foolish back then," Edwards says of his early days on "All Things Considered." But then he quickly points out that listeners still send him chicken soup when he's dragging. Somehow that old standard for closeness no longer seems relevant in NPR's newsroom, where things have clearly shifted from personal to practical.

We don't have 250 million people tuning in. We have 6 million, but I think we have the 6 that listen. We're going to find all the people who are serious about the world, and they'll be our listeners. But we can't pretend that anything close to a majority of the country is going to be serious about the world.   —Bob Edwards, host of "Morning Edition"

Edwards still goes out of his way to put a face on his listening audience. Every month he travels to a member station for a fund-raising breakfast or speech and "finds out what listeners are talking about," he says. "I know what these people look like. I see the same people in every town. Some of them are real button-down lawyers and some of them are Euell Gibbons in flannel shirts and suspenders. 'Don't even have a television,' they say, and I believe it."

He points to places like Alaska —"which is so beautiful even God must think so"— as an example of where public radio still plays a very intimate role in listeners' lives. "They have a program out there called the 'Daily Mail,'" he says, then stages a mock announcement: "'John in Tuckatoo: The plane will be in on Thursday.' That's how they communicate up there." But that's up there, not here on the continental United States where 99 percent of Americans live.

Old-timers like Edwards, Stamberg, and Alex Chadwick continue to cling to that chicken soup connection that they built up when the network was young. But both NPR and the founding cast have moved into middle age now, and management and news staffers have found themselves connecting to listeners on an entirely different level.

More and more the personal touch pops up in programming outside the regular news shows. "Morning Edition" might air a straight news item on the invasion of Kuwait, but then in a special call-in later in the day, the network would ask listeners to discuss the event. The call-in weekday program, "Talk of the Nation," sprang out of the tremendous phone response NPR received during the Gulf War. John Hockenberry launched the program brandishing his trademark wit. He brought in people like Salman Rushdie to discuss *The Satanic Verses* or experts on events in Eastern Europe, then opened the phone lines for irreverent discussions with callers. "The public radio audience is very active," he says. "That's where 'Talk of the Nation' exists, at the point of engagement. And that's great."

The call-in also allowed him to explore the one characteristic he and many others believe has always sustained NPR—curiosity.

"I'm a wiseass on the air; always looking for the one-liners," he says, "and

Talk of flowers, as well as baseball, gave a special lightness of spirit and charm to the weekly dialogues between Red Barber and Bob Edwards, shown above in his garden.

87

John Hockenberry is curious by nature. He says, "I think curiosity is one of the least threatening and most motivating emotions you can express on the air."

I'm curious. I think curiosity is one of the least threatening and most motivating emotions you can express on the air."

But Hockenberry left the show and NPR in the summer of 1992 to become a correspondent for ABC News in New York. The fact that Robert Siegel, one of NPR's top guns, left his seat as host of "All Things Considered" to replace Hockenberry indicates that the network considers the call-in show something worth sustaining—despite a slow sign-up rate among member stations.

In an interview that took place before his announced departure, Hockenberry expressed concerns about the general drift of NPR programming. He felt the news shows had lost their "chummy feel," and programs like "Talk of the Nation" were not enough to bridge the gap. "NPR has started to think of itself as a modular news service, you know, where all the newscasts are six minutes at the top of the hour, and a station can take all of them or none of them," he said.

"I remember this editorial meeting for 'ATC' back in [the early 1980s]. The discussion was about some story issue, and the conclusion was, *No, we are not going to be a news program. What we don't want to be is a news program.* The idea of that conversation being engaged in today is silly."

Bob Ferrante, executive producer for morning news, believes that such changes are just part of NPR's maturing process. "Obviously the audience we attracted as a result of going to hard news has been phenomenal," he says, citing the huge number of listeners NPR gained in the last two years, in large part because of its Gulf War coverage. "It's like the clothes we wore as younger people," he adds. "Now we think 'Jesus, how did we ever?' But at the time, boy, did we think we were cool."

Interestingly enough, some NPR fans seem relieved that the network has shirked the more neighborly approach. "Scott Simon has a major problem," one letter writer told public station WFPL in Louisville, Kentucky. "He considers *himself* the reason for the program he directs. He appears to me to use his time on air as a time of private self-indulgence. . . . All Simon is required to do is present the issue and the person or persons involved in an objective manner. Just the facts. . . . *I don't care what he thinks. I only care to know what is going on,*" he concluded indignantly—a hard news listener for an information-laden era. He makes Bill Siemering sound like a doting grandfather when Siemering makes the soft complaint that "NPR doesn't quite have that same personable quality to it." Indeed, the letter writer's statement stands in stark contrast to the stricken look on Siemering's face when the former program director heard that Simon planned to leave the network. Simon's one of the few left who still project "a personality, not just a voice," Siemering says.

Somehow the NPR staff of the 1970s did manage to place an audio signature on the network's shows that it has never completely shaken. Fans hear it every time Bob Edwards marks another birthday or chats with characters like sports legend Red Barber, who died in October 1992 after years of entertaining "Morning Edition" listeners with his homilies on sports, cats, and gardens. And sometimes the personal touch just springs up unexpectedly in the middle of an otherwise standard newscast.

Like the day Cokie Roberts's dog barked through her live report for "Morning Edition" on the troubled state of the American economy. Since Roberts also reports for ABC News and "The MacNeil/Lehrer NewsHour," she rarely has time to make it downtown to the radio network's recording studio for her conversations with Bob Edwards. Instead she uses a special high-quality telephone line at her house.

Listeners began calling with questions as soon as Roberts got off the air.

"Was that a dog I heard in the newsroom?" asked one man from Salisbury, Maryland.

"Is the basset hound a Democrat or Republican?" a Walton, Illinois, fan wanted to know.

One listener from Indiana said he "liked the piece. My only problem was they never gave the dog the microphone. I always thought that in America any son-of-a-bitch had a right to speak his mind."

A few days later "Morning Edition" aired a special three-minute segment: "The Mysterious Barking Dog."

"Well, Bob," said Roberts, "our dirty little secret is out. Most mornings when you and I have our conversations, I must admit it, I am in my very discreet nightie."

Cokie Roberts says that radio "is the most fun medium. People hear what you're saying. They aren't disturbed or distracted by the visual image."

"But until this week we did not hear from your four-legged roommate," the host replied.

"Well, my dog, Abner, is a lovely basset hound, about four-years old; brown and white with long ears and sad eyes," she explained. "And he has been very, very eager to make his debut. It's been a difficult task to keep him away from the microphone. This dog wants to be a radio dog."

Even though Roberts left full-time radio work years ago, she still considers radio "the most fun medium. People hear what you're saying. They aren't disturbed or distracted by the visual image.

"When you read quotes in print it's like the rest of the page, but in radio that's not the case. Sometimes the most telling sound in radio is a pause.

"I did a piece recently where I asked young people who they think of when they think of a Democratic leader. One after another said, "Hmmmm, well, let me see." I left a long note for the tapecutters, 'Don't cut these pauses.' They said so much about where the Democratic Party is."

Perhaps it's the distinctive qualities of radio and the lack of creative programming on commercial stations that make some people so jittery about any changes at NPR. If the network leans too far toward hard news or market-driven programming, who will be left to air the unexpected?

This dark view fails to take into account the growing success of American Public Radio and the emerging presence of independent producers at the local station level. But, more importantly, it also undercuts the crucial role that listeners play at NPR. They—more than hosts and producers—give the network its spirit.

"We don't have 250 million tuning in," says Edwards. "We have 6 million, but I think we have the 6 that listen. We're going to find all the people who are serious about the world, and they'll be our listeners and that will be it."

So a distinct few listen, and in return they expect distinct programming. They're remarkably vocal about every step that NPR takes. It's *their* network. "Morning Edition" and "All Things Considered" are *their* shows.

"NPR matters to people's lives," says Alex Chadwick. "That derives from and leads to a sense of possibility in programming." The question remains, he adds, whether NPR can continue to really matter to people's lives in "a way that is tremendously rewarding."

NPR fans will be sure to let the network know if it doesn't.

CHAPTER EIGHT

The New York Times
of the Airwaves

For more than twenty years listeners have tuned in to NPR news programs to hear Susan Stamberg talk about cranberry sauce recipes, Noah Adams tell of atrocities in Sarajevo, or Bob Edwards banter with a reporter covering an offbeat story. The voices may change, but on a day-to-day basis "All Things Considered" and "Morning Edition" fall like a security blanket over many Americans' day.

But if fans could listen to a random sampling of some old tapes of these two shows from the 1970s, 1980s, and 1990s, they'd hear just how much NPR's approach to news has changed: a quicker pace, more foreign news, more news and less chat—period. The shifts were all part of the network's metamorphosis from a shoestring public radio operation into a primary news source that can compete with the best in broadcast and print media.

As the man holding the reins of this more aggressive animal, President Doug Bennet hardly abides by Bob Edwards's statement that NPR should be happy if it reaches 6 million listeners "who are serious about the world." Once he felt secure that the network had survived its brush with bankruptcy, Bennet began pushing hard for a programming agenda that centered around two primary goals: to build and broaden audience.

In the world of commercial media this would seem like a given not worth pinpointing in a statement of purpose. Of course a television network or newspaper wants to reach as many people as it can. A bigger audience usually translates into more influence and more money. But to many hard-liners in the world of public broadcasting, Bennet's objectives seemed crass and too market-driven. They feared that NPR would become too taken with audience numbers instead of new ideas. Bennet shrugs off such criticism and calls it a "superficial reading" of his agenda. Public radio cannot sustain its legitimacy, he says, if it fails to reach for a wider audience. Such efforts do not have to preclude "creating things that are fresh," he adds.

When he arrived in 1983, Bennet felt the answer to many of NPR's problems lay in breaking away from old standards, "however good or bad they might have been—and taking up a new standard, a new definition of what our service looked like. The first big step was to start something new—anything to show that the network could *expand* after all that it had lost during the financial crisis."

Former "Morning Edition" producer Jay Kernis teamed with Scott Simon to create a two-hour program for Saturday mornings that they knew had to be "the sixth day of 'All Things Considered' but different," says Kernis. "Weekend Edition" fell right in line with NPR's old style of news programming: personality driven, often irreverent, and leisurely paced. It marked a new beginning but not a new concept.

"I'll never forget starting the Saturday show," says Bennet. "It was enormously important symbolically to start something again. Once you could, then it became possible to talk seriously about an agenda."

The program was an instant success, due in large part to the fervent response Simon elicited from his fans. They swamped NPR with letters praising his sensitivity and finely written scripts and wailed when he left for NBC in the summer of 1992.

Even the behind-the-scenes staff had a lost-puppy look on Simon's final day. Unlike "Morning Edition," where producers, editors, and directors rarely stay more than a year or two, most of the people on "Weekend Edition" started with Simon in 1987. Some even followed the host from his earlier job as Chicago bureau chief. Staffers like director Neva Grant or technician Rick Rarey had spent the last five years orchestrating Scott Simon first, the show second.

During Simon's final broadcast on July 25, 1992, Rarey roamed the control room with a bottle of saline solution and a box of Kleenex. He kept sprinkling mock tears into his eyes, then waving the tissue box at Simon and others. They all laughed, told stories about old shows, then fell sadly quiet when the host's taped goodbye came on the air. They planned to return to the control room the

Doug Bennet (opposite page) is a talented Washington hand and accomplished public servant with a Harvard Ph.D. to boot. Critics still say, "But he was never a journalist." Scott Simon (left) has a voice and an offbeat and sensitive style that attract devoted followers.

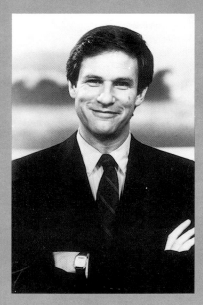

Quality, NPR's hallmark, derives from a mix of talents in various places: Joyce Davis on the foreign desk, Robert Krulwich (now at CBS) on business, Maria Hinojosa reporting from New York (top to bottom); commentator Daniel Schorr (opposite).

following Saturday, they said, but they all looked as though they'd just lost a job.

Simon described his own departure as a "sabbatical," which leaves the door to the radio network open just in case his job as host of NBC television's weekend "Today" show doesn't pan out. In the interim, old-timers like Alex Chadwick, Neal Conan, and Susan Stamberg—each of whom fits easily within the NPR tradition of hosts who project personalities as well as the news—will rotate as "visiting" hosts.

Even as "Weekend Edition" relied on NPR's old formula for success, "All Things Considered" and "Morning Edition" had already made changes that purposely broke with many of those traditions. They became less personality driven, making them less susceptible to the empty feeling caused by the departure of a star host like Stamberg. The news editors seemed more intent on having the story itself be the hook that held listeners, which in turn made it easier to appeal to and sustain a wider audience.

The changes were most noticeable on "All Things Considered," which transformed itself into a "newsmagazine that was served by a Washington bureau news operation and a national desk," says John Hockenberry, who started at the network in 1981 in the newscaster unit. "Suddenly reporters didn't work for 'ATC'; they worked for NPR News, and NPR News was delivered to 'ATC' and 'Morning Edition' in pieces."

He pauses for a moment, then launches into a monologue on audience like a man who thinks about it in his sleep: "They'll tell you that they've been gaining audience all along and that stations like it. I think that they have been gaining audience based on an earlier reputation, and they also have gained audience because the rest of radio is deteriorating. However quickly NPR is becoming more bland, the rest of radio is just dropping off the map.

"The question of getting audience is a different one than why do you exist. If the reason why you exist is just to get audience, you might as well do phone sex all day."

Bennet finds all this nostalgia for the old style, which he describes as "precious, self-indulgent, and cutesy," rather ridiculous. "When you hear some white male saying [the news programs] aren't as good as they were in the old days, they really mean they're not the same, and that's good," he says.

Member stations have a lot to do with the changes. Once they were served the user-friendly format of "Morning Edition," with eight breaks for local traffic, weather, and fund-raising plugs, they became increasingly impatient with the idea of an unbroken, slow-paced, ninety-minute newsmagazine. "In recent years there's been a lot of pressure on 'All Things Considered' to allow stations to come in more frequently," says executive producer Ellen Weiss. "There's a lot of legitimacy to their argument. Programming costs a lot of money, and stations do the underwriting. There's not a lot of opportunity to break into the show. It's really two worlds colliding. The stations have definite needs, but the show has very definite ideas."

In the past NPR ignored blustering managers because it knew no public

radio station could afford to drop the network's flagship show. Outside of "Morning Edition," "ATC" draws the most listeners and the most acclaim. But the desire to build audience met up with the growing power of individual stations. The two currents created a whirlpool that has edged NPR news programs towards a crisper, more practical style.

Now the network can shuffle hosts in and out of "All Things Considered" with little concern for the overall integrity of the program, because *what* the show says has become much more important than *who* says it. Noah Adams can experiment with a variety show in Minnesota, then return to his old seat without missing a beat. Robert Siegel can move to the relatively obscure call-in program "Talk of the Nation" while former "Weekend ATC" host Lynn Neary quietly takes his place. Linda Wertheimer can play musical chairs in the three-host rotation and still have time to cover the presidential campaign. Fans no longer flood the network with mail because some voice has gone away.

It's all part of NPR's altered vision for news, which no one articulates better than Bob Ferrante: "What confuses people is that National Public Radio is a news service. We don't own a station. We're in the marketplace now. If they don't think we're doing a good job, they can buy something else. I don't want to risk sounding too commercial, but we do have to be sought after or we'll become insular. We'll begin to think that what we're doing is God's work. We're not doing God's work. We're doing the news."

The question remains, says Alex Chadwick, whether NPR can also still "do" alternative voices. "Today 'alternative voices' means we're going to find someone who's proabortion and someone who's antiabortion and let them talk for ten minutes, and that's good," he says. "We should do that. But that's not the

Distinctive people, distinctive voices in a variety of roles: Neal Conan, Lynn Neary, Brenda Wilson, Robert Siegel, and Linda Wertheimer (left to right).

Behind the scenes makes a difference: former Vice President for News Adam Powell (above), his successor, Bill Buzenberg (opposite far right), with senior producer Art Silverman.

'alternative voices' that I have in mind. NPR should be a place where people can get conventional news, but it should also be a place where things can get on the air that not everyone will like."

Bennet immediately turns the tables on critics like Chadwick. He claims that when he arrived as president in 1983, many of the white staffers felt "they were committed to worthy goals and so it was impossible for them to be racist" or narrow-minded. "But that was not correct."

To achieve the kind of diversity he wanted for the network Bennet decided NPR needed an aggressive affirmative action program. So he hired Adam Powell, son of the famous Harlem Congressman Adam Clayton Powell, as vice president for news. It was a move that set in motion a chain of events that irrevocably altered the news division. "The Powell period was significant but extremely difficult," Bennet says. "It was a painful period for him, for me, for everyone. It showed how much work we had to do on the whole issue."

Powell made a concerted effort to hire minority journalists from radio stations and newspapers, including three hosts, two newscasters, and correspondent Phyllis Crockett. Most of his hires slipped right into the scheme of things, but not all. In particular, staffers on the domestic desk began to chafe under the changes. Many editors and producers felt the inexperience of some of the new appointees damaged the overall news effort. Powell attributed some of their discomfort to "ingrained institutional racism," but such counterarguments did not offset the division's sinking morale. By the time Bill Buzenberg left his post as London correspondent to replace Powell in 1989, the domestic desk had essentially collapsed under the strain brought about by constant infighting.

"We were supplying about 60 to 70 percent of all the news aired," says foreign editor Cadi Simon. "I'm talking about the period of '87 through mid-way 1990. For three, almost four, years, the foreign desk filled most of the void."

At the time Bennet told a *Washington Post* reporter that Powell's personnel changes had been "disruptive" but necessary. Certainly no other major media organization in the United States today can match the diversity of NPR's newsroom staff, which is one-third minority and 51 percent women. "One friend told me over lunch that he thought I was president of the most important female-dominated institution in the country," Bennet says.

But when Buzenberg set about rebuilding the domestic news division, he had to make an applicant's color or sex a secondary consideration. "Making the programming work had to be the highest goal," he says. To streamline the news operation, Buzenberg had to cut some narrowly focused ethnic programs like "Latin File," which reached only thirty stations; but he offset the loss by incorporating a lot of that material directly into "Morning Edition" and "ATC."

"We concentrated our resources and put them where the largest audience is," says Buzenberg. "I think it helped with diversity" because it placed the work of minority producers, editors, hosts, and reporters directly into the news mainstream. "We still can't say, 'Gee, we did it,' when it comes to affirmative action," he adds, "but we've come a long way."

In addition to broadening the makeup of its staff, NPR has also fought the tendency to become insular by funneling more resources into foreign news. Listeners who first heard NPR while roaming the dial for information on the Gulf War seemed genuinely shocked to find that America's public radio network had a significant presence overseas. What was NPR doing with eight reporters in the Middle East, some of whom had as much as ten years of experience in the region?

The network first turned a serious eye to international coverage in 1978, when it sent Robert Siegel to England to open a London bureau; however, it didn't really commit major resources to a foreign story until Israel invaded Lebanon in 1982. The financial problems unearthed in 1983 stalled overseas efforts, but NPR picked up the pace again with its coverage of the overthrow of President Ferdinand Marcos in the Philippines in 1986.

Cadi Simon believes that story marked a turning point for the foreign desk because it established a form of coverage that involved "more than one person and treated the story like an ongoing news event rather than just coming back and gathering tape." NPR took the same approach for later big stories, like the student uprising in China, the destruction of the Berlin Wall, and the breakup of the Soviet Union. "The coverage of the Gulf War did not happen in a void. It came out of a network that was established, a mind-set that we had come into," says Simon.

NPR's take on Operation Desert Storm put on parade all that the network has become and plans to be in the 1990s and beyond. As always, it offered more analysis, longer stories, and a more personal angle than television, which captured the breaking-news department with its unnerving pictures. The ingredients for the NPR recipe remained the same, but the measurements had clearly been altered: less sugar, more salt and flour.

The best programming, such as the February 2, 1991, broadcast of "Weekend Edition," managed to showcase both the apple pie and the main course. Commentator Daniel Schorr began the show with a scathing critique of some of the biggest glitches in the Allied war plan: too many deaths by friendly fire, too many Iraqi air force jets making it to Iran, and so on. Alex Chadwick, who sat in for Scott Simon stationed in Saudi Arabia, countered with comments on what seemed to be going right: cleaning up the oil spills in the Persian Gulf, gaining control of the skies, and knocking down Scuds.

Then the show broke to Simon, who delivered one of those dry press pool reports that all journalists in the Middle East had to resort to because of American military censorship. But he quickly transformed his predictable, newsy broadcast into a personal essay with an unusual aside about forty-year-old reporters chumming around with eighteen-year-old soldiers.

"In just a few days we may all have to remember and respect the fact that though we were assigned to the same territory, we have distinctly different missions," he reported. "For some reason nothing made that difference plainer to me this week than the fact that the soldiers are offered paper cups of cartoon-colored Fruit Loop cereal for breakfast. It helped remind me that most reporters are too old for Fruit Loops and cannot cover this war as though it were the simple bashing of bad by good like after-breakfast cartoons. And it also seemed sad that people eating a children's breakfast should be fortifying themselves for war."

"Weekend Edition" then cut back to an offbeat thirty-second item by Alex Chadwick on Israelis who decorated the cardboard boxes that carried their gas masks. "In an effort to make things as normal as possible, the Israelis have started painting designs on the cardboard boxes that contain gas masks issued by the government," he said. "Some have bright yellow happy-face stickers, others have polka dots—there are even crocheted slipcovers. Since last Sunday there have been reports that some of the boxes feature cut-out and glued-on copies of the 'Doonesbury' Desert Storm comic strip."

During the 1970s and perhaps even the 1980s, NPR probably would have handled Chadwick's vignette like a full-fledged personal interest story, complete with interviews with crocheting Jewish mothers and sticker-crazed children. Instead, the news program handed the airtime to John Hockenberry, who reported on people fleeing Tel Aviv.

Few listeners know that Hockenberry works out of a wheelchair. A car accident during his college days at the University of Chicago left him paralyzed from the waist down. He found the wheels of his chair couldn't fit through the doors of an air-raid shelter in Tel Aviv, so he sat outside the room and typed up his scripts with a gas mask on. When he decided to track the plight of the Kurds struggling in the mountains between Iraq and Turkey, he left his wheelchair in a taxi and made the nine-hour trek strapped on the back of a donkey.

On February 2, 1991, he was following the emotional trail of people torn between making a stand in Tel Aviv or moving out of Scud range. One woman drew a parallel between the Jews who stayed in Germany during World War II and those fleeing Saddam Hussein. "Look what happened to them," she said. "Why should I sit and wait in Tel Aviv when I can leave?"

A general's daughter chastised the local politicians who ridiculed those who wanted to run. "Bravery should not be a prison," she said. "Fear is an individual thing." The microphone picked up children in the background and the edgy shuffling of people trying to contain their panic.

The layered approach of this program reflects all the elements that made NPR's Gulf War coverage unique, but the weekday shows only occasionally

The Gulf War: Scuds, Patriots, and NPR. Extraordinary coverage from (clockwise from upper left) John Hockenberry, Scott Simon, Deborah Wang, John Ydstie, John Ogulnik and Linda Wertheimer, Deborah Amos, and Neal Conan (center).

reached such artistic heights. Because much of the war happened on the "Morning Edition" watch, it aired most of the key stories. Its punctual format provided an altogether different service for information-starved listeners.

While a long list of reporters filled NPR's airtime during the war, most staffers generally point to Deborah Amos and Deborah Wang as standouts. Edwards calls Wang "the Queen of the Briefings."

"They'd [government and military officials] come prepared to do their public relations tour," he says, "and Wang would shake them up. She was so good we thought we'd lose her" to a commercial network with more money.

While most of Wang's stories came straight from the hip, Amos strove to add a personal touch. "By the time of the Iraqi invasion of Kuwait I had traveled to just about every corner of the region," she writes in *Lines in the Sand*, her book on what went on behind the scenes during the Gulf War. "I had always made it a point to mix the political analysis and war reporting with the personal stories of people who lived in the region. I wanted to convey that they were people who washed dishes, drove the children to school, ate dinner, and worried about the future."

Her reporting ran the gamut from standard interviews with soldiers to discussions on the possible consequences of the language barrier between American and Arab soldiers working together in the field. When asked to cite her favorite story, she replies, "A piece I did on an American woman who was crying about having to leave her six-month-old baby behind to go to war and looking at Saudi women in their black chadors and saying, 'Hey, maybe they're right.' I tried to deal with some very tough personal issues."

What confuses people is that National Public Radio is a news service. We don't own a station. We're in the marketplace now. We don't want to risk sounding too commercial, but we do have to be sought after, or we'll become insular. We'll begin to think that what we're doing is God's work. We're not doing God's work. We're doing the news. —*Bob Ferrante, executive producer for morning news*

But NPR's shimmering moments remain tempered by charges that the network's overall coverage proved much too stiff and conservative. "I didn't just hear that from my radical lefty friends," says Hockenberry. "In some ways the Gulf War coverage is an indication that NPR has gone completely from being a quirky, experimental, interesting place to being an organ of record where interesting and quirky are sidelines."

Ellen Weiss agrees that NPR relied too heavily on staged news conferences and the pap of military and government officials during the first few weeks of the war, but then she began working the phones and brought in more offbeat commentators, like American linguist Noam Chomsky. Hockenberry feels that Weiss was one of the few producers who snapped out of it and really tried to do something different. "I didn't want listeners to tune in to 'ATC' and always hear what they expected to hear," she says.

No matter how hard she tried, Weiss never could have produced a program offbeat enough to appease all NPR fans unless she sacrificed the news division's

commitment to objectivity. Bob Edwards and other longtime NPR staffers think that many listeners assumed that public radio would be the leading conduit for antiwar, antigovernment voices, because it had established a reputation for airing dissident voices when it first went on the air near the close of the Vietnam War.

But NPR's obscurity during that era made it difficult for the network to tap into the establishment. No big-name politician or military official wanted to waste time trying to get on the public radio system. But NPR no longer had a second-row seat at the table of mass media when Saddam Hussein decided to roll into Kuwait. Getting on "Morning Edition" meant just as much to public officials as getting on "CBS News with Dan Rather" or on the front page of *The New York Times*. Now the network could line up Noam Chomsky *and* Vice President Dan Quayle.

In the past, right-wing politicians, think tanks, and conservative journalists

Happy faces from border to border. The happiest one may be Alex Chadwick's, as he visits the children of Vietnam and shares insights with NPR listeners about life in that country — once the center of American reporting and now too often forgotten.

Ultimately good reporters and good editors depend on good producers such as Ellen Weiss to choose wisely among available stories, to encourage those approaches that may be a little different, a little chancy, yet still manage to maintain balance.

have viewed NPR's liberal reputation as the network's Achilles heel and have sent their barbs in that direction whenever they wanted to undermine an NPR story or public broadcasting in general. The normally left-leaning *New Republic* ran an editorial in 1986 entitled, "All Things Distorted," which lambasted NPR for a favorable story it did on the contras in Nicaragua. Right-wing organizations like Accuracy in Media and the Heritage Foundation still keep careful tabs on how many liberal commentators the network uses and how much airtime it delegates to stories on homosexuality, prochoice, and other left-of-center causes. They use the results to bolster their argument that public broadcasting should not receive federal funding.

NPR's Gulf War coverage elicited few complaints from the right—perhaps a sign that the network has finally shaken old stereotypes of itself and been recognized as the neutral, legitimate news source it has always tried to be. The network's war reporting also elicited a change of heart among normally tightfisted station managers, who willingly raised an additional $750,000 to help NPR cover the cost of keeping reporters in Israel, Saudi Arabia, and Jordan.

All in all, NPR traversed an unbelievable amount of ground during the war on just $1.8 million. It proved once again that radio can carry farther and move more efficiently than television. As legal affairs reporter Nina Totenberg says, "The Gulf War coverage proved unmistakably that NPR could do as well as a multibillion-dollar network and in some ways better. We were in the big leagues and no longer an alternative."

Totenberg as much as anyone embodies both the journalistic skills that brought NPR out of the shadows and the attitude that will direct the network for the next decade. As a beat reporter she's never felt she should offer alternative views. She reported Watergate and the Iran-contra hearings in a straightforward manner. When she broke the story about Supreme Court nominee Douglas Ginsberg's pot-smoking past, she pulled no punches but also took no sides. *Vanity Fair* labeled her "Queen of the Leaks" in 1992, which had little to do with whatever personality she projects over the air and everything to do with the stories she regularly uncovers.

Of course, the story of all Totenberg stories remains the leak that almost brought down Clarence Thomas. On October 6, 1992, Totenberg told "Weekend Edition" listeners in a bland, direct voice that a law professor named Anita Hill had indicated in an affidavit that Supreme Court nominee Clarence Thomas had asked her out socially while she worked for him in Washington, D.C. He "refused to accept her explanation that she did not think it appropriate to go out with her boss," Totenberg reported. "The relationship became even more strained when Thomas, in work situations, began to discuss sex. On these occasions he would call her into his office to discuss work. Thomas, after a brief work discussion, would, quote, 'turn the conversation around to discussions about his sexual interests.' His conversations, she said, were vivid. He spoke about sex acts he had seen in pornographic films involving such things as women having sex with animals and films involving group sex and rape scenes.

He talked about pornographic material depicting individuals with large penises and breasts . . ."

A *Newsday* reporter in New York also broke the story, but only Totenberg managed to secure an actual copy of the affidavit. Radio proved an ideal medium for Anita Hill's first step into the public arena. She didn't have to face a camera, and her taped comments projected her tentative, yet articulate, voice in a way a printed quotation never could.

"Well, he made a statement [pause] about his behavior," she told Totenberg, "that [pause] it was [the word fades softly here] if I ever did disclose it—that it would be enough to ruin his career."

Totenberg not only snagged the story, but also nailed down a comment from Sen. Joseph Biden that underscored his blindness to the larger issue of sexual harassment raised by Hill's testimony. "Character is not the issue here," he told Totenberg with an edge in his voice. "This is about what he believes, not who he is."

She later reported on Biden's decision not to tell most of his colleagues about the Hill affidavit until the night of the Senate committee vote. Instead of having a closed-door discussion with Hill, instead of investigating, the Senator chose to ignore the whole story. That's when some unidentified congressional staffer decided to drop Totenberg a line. When asked by a *Vanity Fair* reporter if such leaks are common, she laughed and said Washington's "a sieve."

An enraged Republican Party and a jealous media establishment soon turned on Totenberg and began investigating her past with a vengeance. The tension reached the breaking point after an appearance she made with Sen. Alan Simpson on ABC's "Nightline" during the Hill-Thomas hearings. "Let's not pretend you're objective here," he snorted at her on the show.

Afterwards the two of them tangled on the way out the door. "Did you ever read the code of professional ethics?" he shouted. "How about the part that says you respect the privacy and dignity of those you deal with?"

Accounts differ on what Totenberg sent back in return. "You big shit. Fuck you," say several sources—an account she doesn't deny. "You are an evil, ugly, bitter person, and all your colleagues hate you," say other sources, an account she does refute, but with a laugh.

Later that week *The Wall Street Journal* ran an editorial that dug up plagiarism charges levied against Totenberg in 1972 when she was a print

For a reporter, getting the story, no matter how good, can rarely change the way a whole nation looks at a problem. Nina Totenberg's work on the Clarence Thomas confirmation hearings did.

"Fresh Air," an honored cultural affairs "magazine," is Terry Gross's baby: conceived by her as a student in the sixties, nurtured by her on WBFO, and still growing under her artful hand at WHYY in Philadelphia. For 1.5 million listeners each week, it is a cultural feast.

knew he "had to find a different way to do things," he says. "Many stations were anxious to produce their own programs. It occurred to me to use NPR resources to help stations create programs they could run on the network. I saw it as the next step towards maturity for the stations."

Instead of producing costly specials like "A Question of Place," Boal figured the network could buy material from stations in Minnesota, Los Angeles, St. Louis, Boston, Philadelphia, and elsewhere. All it needed to offer was a little money, a lot of encouragement, and satellite space. In 1984 it was still unclear whether the network could do even that. "NPR's expenditure on cultural programming had been cut way back," says Bennet. "What was left was what people could give us, which was fine, but it wasn't terrific." The bargain basement approach left the network with a cultural programming agenda more akin to a garage sale than a museum.

The following year someone from the Corporation for Public Broadcasting pulled Bennet aside and whispered in his ear, "No more money for arts programming." Now NPR not only lacked the resources to buy decent material, but also the funds for a bare-bones staff to oversee promotion and distribution of what little it could pull in on the fly. So Bennet and Boal launched a fund-raising campaign.

"People had to come to grips with whether they wanted cultural programming on radio," says Boal. "The problem was that we had no political power within the structure, because most people in management at NPR were interested in news. I just pulled out all the stops in the arts community to keep it going."

He unplugged $8 million in just a few months—enough money to sustain the department and develop "Performance Today," a subdued successor to "The Sunday Show." The department continues to rely more heavily than news on outside funding and on programs produced by member stations.

> We're scared to look our own demons in the face, but it's awfully interesting to look at them through the distance that art or someone else's life affords.
> —*Terry Gross, host of "Fresh Air"*

Terry Gross's hour-long cultural magazine, "Fresh Air," produced by WHYY in Philadelphia, remains among the most popular of this kind of show. A small woman with a voice like deep water, Gross conceived of the program while still a student in Buffalo, New York, in the 1960s. She eventually aired a three-hour version on Bill Siemering's old station, WBFO, then took the show with her when she joined WHYY in 1975.

By the time NPR picked up "Fresh Air" for national distribution in 1987, Gross had already established herself as a leading chronicler of American cultural life. Like an audio encyclopedia, her show offers an unpredictable mix of interviews with artists and critiques of everything from books and movies to poster art.

As an interviewer Gross rarely goes for the jugular, choosing instead to probe more introspective topics, like author John Updike's love for faces. "A dermal sin," he called it. Or she might discuss "the lowly role of women in American detective fiction" with British crime novelist P. D. James.

Even though 1.5 million NPR fans tune in to "Fresh Air" each week, not everyone embraces Gross's East Coast style. One station in Alaska dropped "Fresh Air" because it featured "one lesbian, feminist, stand-up comic from Greenwich Village too many," says the manager. "The show was simply too eastern and too urban."

Gross remains enthused about her own show after seventeen years, partly because she sees each interview as an opportunity to explore something in herself. "We're scared to look our own demons in the face," she told a reporter from the *Washington Journalism Review,* "but it's awfully interesting to look at them through the distance that art or someone else's life affords." The wonders of satellite transmission allow her to keep a comfortable distance between the people she quizzes and herself. Not unlike Ted Koppel on "Nightline," she finds "it a lot easier to ask tough questions if you're not face to face."

To truly diversify its programming, however, NPR had to break away from the "eastern, urban" art cycle that "Fresh Air" represents and bring in something

that could never be compared to Ted Koppel. It landed on Sean Barlow's "Afropop Worldwide," which airs music and storytellers from Brazil, Ghana, Kenya, Colombia, and anywhere else that Barlow and Cameroon host Georges Collinet can find an African beat.

In a marketing twist that underscores the power shift between NPR and member stations, Barlow first won local managers' support for his independent music project by airing at a public radio conference tapes of material he'd collected on a trip to Ghana and Cameroon. "We really worked hard," he says, "so that everyone who was there that was a decision maker on the local level would know about the series and get excited about it." He stimulated demand first, then delivered the end product to the network, which snatched it up immediately.

Since 1987, "Afropop Worldwide" has fea-

Stories and music combine to make "Afropop Worldwide" an uncommon attraction for NPR listeners who applaud the work of host Georges Collinet (opposite) and the talent he attracts, including (from left to right) Miriam Makeba, Annette Konan, Thomas Mapfumo, El Grande Cuba, and Omar Peine.

tured artists like Gilbert Gil from Brazil, and "the Lion of Zimbabwe," Thomas Mapfumo, who performed in New Orleans in 1991 to "a packed, sweaty house of public radio people," says Barlow. "He just blew them away." More than 200 managers have picked up the program, a significant draw considering many of NPR's 450 member stations air only classical music.

"But it's not just the music," says Barlow. "It's also the stories and the storytellers. We know our listeners are curious about the world. They listen to 'All Things Considered.' They listen to 'Morning Edition.' They follow world events. . . . The show is really a vehicle for telling the stories of underreported places through music, which is the best bridge possible."

When "Afropop Worldwide" sponsored a concert for WBUR in Boston, African-Americans from the local community volunteered to teach their native dances to a predominantly white crowd. "We like to do that kind of thing to give stations the chance to be catalysts for creating exciting cross-cultural events in the community," says Barlow. "That's when the radio series can transcend into a different medium and different experiences, and that's very exciting."

Such successes have convinced many people at NPR, including Doug Bennet, that the network's potential as a builder of bridges in a multicultural society can best be realized through song and story, not news. Only the unbiased draw of art can erode many of the boundaries that exist between different races and ethnic groups in the United States. Public stations that air a wide variety of cultural programming could become educators, mediators, perhaps even peacemakers.

The network took its first definitive steps toward a cross-cultural agenda when it sent Steve Rathe out to find material for "Folk Festival USA" and "Jazz Alive." Today NPR continues its tradition in rhythm-and-blues through the weekly series "BluesStage," produced by CEIB Productions, Inc., in Brooklyn. The show covers a wide spectrum, from gritty, out-of-the way locales like the B. K. Lounge in Rochester, to center stage with a star like B. B. King.

A 1992 special on King's performance at the San Francisco Blues Festival showcased the program's ability to do an old trick well. Host Ruth Brown, a Grammy-award-winning R & B star, didn't just plunge NPR listeners into King's concert. She trained the audience's ear first by sketching a biography of King, then playing excerpts from some of his earlier concerts. During a 1950s version of "The Thrill Is Gone," King tugged so intensely on the strings of his guitar—the famous "Lucille"—that you just had to stop and listen to the story of love and loss. After hearing that excerpt, it becomes clear that the B. B. King of the 1990s is a different man—happier, more stable, but somehow also less embracing.

Music alone will not get NPR into every cranny it wants to reach, so it has also picked up programs like "Car Talk," a sixty-minute weekly call-in show produced by WBUR in Boston that's part comedy routine, part auto-repair clinic. Someone with a leaky carburetor or faulty starter phones Tom and Ray Magliozzi, who own an auto-repair shop in Boston, and the brothers try to solve the problem. Along the way they use America's love/hate relationship with the automobile to fuel an incredibly successful stand-up routine. Before Susan Stamberg convinced NPR to take on "Car Talk" in 1987, Bostonians already tuned in to the program as often as they listened to "All Things Considered" and "Morning Edition."

As one *New York Times* reviewer puts it, the hosts use their voices to roll their eyes, shrug their shoulders, and slap their foreheads. With thick Boston accents, they tell a woman that her 1979 Honda Accord is a "chamber pot," or a man that the "Volvo is the poor man's Mercedes because the repair bills will keep you too poor to buy a Mercedes." Most of the humor is done at the expense of foreign cars, but callers aren't above a ribbing now and then. "Boy, we get'em, don't we?" says Ray after a caller hangs up. "He's just a leftover hippie," retorts Tom. "Nothing wrong with that."

"Part of its wonderfulness," says a station manager in San Francisco, "is its Italianness. I think Italians think it's Italian; people who are Jewish think it's Jewish; people who are Greek think it's Greek. Everybody's sitting around the table talking at once."

Listeners tend to have extreme reactions to the noise and, like a favorite

Ruth Brown, talent, host, and teacher on the air, provides unique insight into the musical world of rhythm-and-blues.

B. B. King — holding Lucille, his guitar, in loving embrace — is one of the stars whose music is showcased on "BluesStage."

comic strip, either love it or despise it. "It ties with opera for negative comments," says a station manager in Alaska.

"Car Talk" has certainly won over the management at NPR, which agreed to absorb all the costs of production, a perk it provides for only one other independently produced program, which Peter Pennekamp, vice president for cultural programming, would not identify. He did concede, however, that the cultural department invests as much into "Car Talk" as it does into "everything else combined."

In the end, of course, the network relays such costs back to the stations via the fees it charges for individual programs. The unbundling process, which allowed stations to purchase shows on an individual basis instead of in packages, gave the stations more power over what NPR distributes, but it also made everything more expensive. "We dropped 'Car Talk' for financial reasons," says Carl Jenkins, station manager at KUNI in Cedar Falls, Iowa. "Unbundled it would cost $10,000, and we can't do that." Inadvertently such money problems force smaller stations to narrow, rather than broaden, their program offerings. "There's been a trend toward specializing," says Jenkins. "There are three big tracks: classical, news, and other stuff like blues and jazz. NPR is looking ahead to where stations will have to choose."

Such changes could undermine the network's long-range vision for diversification, but not if NPR can also realize the second part of that plan: to establish more than one public station in each market, with each one catering to a different slice of the local audience. In the meantime, "too many stations are on the cusp of not being able to afford even basic NPR services," Ohio Public Radio President John Perry warned at a conference in Washington, D.C., in 1990.

Increased competition from American Public Radio and even small operations like the left-leaning Pacifica Radio News should help keep NPR's fees down. If programs like "Car Talk" become too pricey, for example, a station can switch to the midwestern humor of APR's quiz and comedy show, "Whad' Ya Know?" with Michael Feldman, which costs stations in bigger markets like New York half what they'd have to pay for "Car Talk." Smaller stations save even more.

Each week Feldman tosses trivia questions at people seated in his live audience in Madison, Wisconsin, or at callers who phone in from across the country. They win prizes like inflatable Oscar Mayer wieners, pink flamingos, and "world-class" skipping stones for correct answers. Sometimes he just chats with contestants about hot topics. During the 1992 presidential campaign he tried to get a different angle on the story by seeking out the person in the audience whose family had suffered the most home visits from candidates.

NPR once carried "Whad' Ya Know?" but gave it up to APR the same year it snagged "Thistle and Shamrock," the weekly Celtic music series, from the Minnesota-based distributor. The network seems more comfortable diversifying through music than through the less predictable world of comedy.

APR also still has its ace card—Garrison Keillor, onetime host of the most successful radio entertainment program in decades, "A Prairie Home Companion." Keillor canceled the show in 1987, even though it still drew at least 4 million listeners every week, so he and his family could travel and live overseas. He returned to the air in 1990 with a new two-hour Saturday evening program, "Garrison Keillor's American Radio Company," now broadcast again out of Minnesota and features Keillor's monologues, the music of American legends like

Listeners care little where programming originates. "Whad' Ya Know," with Michael Feldman (bottom), went from NPR to APR. "Thistle and Shamrock," with Fiona Ritchie (center), moved from APR to NPR. "Car Talk," cohosted by the Magliozzi brothers (opposite), is part of NPR's cultural division, which is run by Peter Pennekamp (top).

117

No public radio program was better known in the 1980s than Garrison Keillor's "A Prairie Home Companion," produced by American Public Radio after NPR, in a classic misjudgment, turned it down as being too regional. Music director Rob Fisher (above) stands by as Ivy Austin prepares to sing.

Aaron Copeland and Fats Waller, and an occasional visit from a Lake Wobegon character stranded in the Big Apple.

After nearly three years on the air, Keillor's new program still only had a weekly audience of about 1.5 million listeners, a large drop from his "A Prairie Home Companion" days. Edgy stations didn't pick it up as quickly as expected, which demonstrates just how difficult the dog-eat-dog market makes it for anyone—superstar or NPR—to experiment with new ideas.

"The stations have opted out of the development triangle," says John Hockenberry. "You can't create a success because they'll only buy into a success." He cites "Car Talk" as an example. "First of all, it took a long time to develop. It was in Boston for ten years. Second, you can't design an entire day around 'Car Talk.' You have to have variety. If what you're looking for is 'Car Talk,' then what you're looking for is 'Lawn Mower Talk,' and 'Toaster Talk.' That's not any way to develop a format."

Pennekamp acknowledges that "'Car Talk' is not the future," because it's talent-based rather than content-based. He worries that cultural programming may continue to drift in that direction even though "that's not as reliable."

But when Hockenberry tried to create the cultural program of the future—the two-hour, broad-based, cultural news show "Heat"—he failed. Indisputably one of the best things to come out of NPR since "Morning Edition," "Heat" tried to dissolve the division between "left brain and right brain," says Hockenberry. "It erased the artificial line between intellectual and creative expression." It tried to add some irreverent kick to the network's middle-age crisis.

During one broadcast in March 1990, Hockenberry spent the first hour celebrating International Women's Day by examining the role of the goddess throughout history. He brought in authors who'd written on the subject, a Harvard divinity professor, and Ann Marie Zappia, a twenty-year veteran waitress from the Rascal House Restaurant, whom he dubbed the "Waitress Goddess."

He continued his blend of wit and weighty comment in the second hour, which focused on the rising death rate among frogs around the world. "Frogs. Frogs. FFFFFrogs." Hockenberry announced. "We're going to do an entire program on the history of frogs. We'll talk to people about why frogs are disappearing. What does it mean?—which is the mission of journalism."

Douglas Kirkpatrick from the American Institute of Aeronautics offered his learned opinion on the jumping abilities of basketball star Michael Jordan and frogs. Zoologist David Wake stepped in with more technical commentary about the growing number of extinct frog species and what that says about the future of the environment. Frog fans extolled the virtues of their favorite frogs, and New Orleans chef Chris Keragorio provided serious advice on the art of cooking and eating frog legs.

After a series of interviews with children concerning proper frog-catching techniques, Hockenberry closed the show with a personal essay that rose like a poem over the entire quirky, insightful, touching, sad, funny broadcast. People have a special affection for frogs, he concluded, because they're "the first creature whose life span can be grasped by a child."

During its eight-month existence, "Heat" also applied this multilayered approach to complex news events, most notably the oil spill that occurred when the tanker *Exxon Valdez* grounded off the coast of Alaska in 1989. In the broadcast equivalent of the wink of an eye, Hockenberry developed a cult following, won radio broadcasting's top award—the Peabody—and saw his program die.

"The loss of 'Heat' proves at least one thing," says Bennet, "that we don't always have enough capacity to sustain innovative programs. 'Heat' was coming on very strong, but we don't have enough of a bridge to subsidize and sustain a program until it's really been tested. Stations' audiences are very conservative about change. [The managers] catch hell from whomever likes what was dropped to make way for the new show. So naturally they're reticent to start something new."

NPR gets two-thirds of its operating budget from fees and dues paid by member stations; the other third must come from outside sources, which "were not willing to take a risk," says Pennekamp, on a show that had to build a following. Corporations and foundations generally feel more comfortable sponsoring ideas with a proven track record.

Such hang-ups lead Hockenberry to ask a crucial question: "What is NPR?

119

Is NPR just an entity that puts out programs that collect an audience and sells funding to programs that already have an audience? Or is it an institution created to explore the consensus or lack of consensus within our society? I think they think they're the latter, but the problem is they're not set up any more to say 'We think this is an interesting program, let's just do it.'"

"We got the money to get ['Heat'] started," says Bennet, "and Hockenberry did a great job; but the assumption from the start was that we must get outside sponsorship to keep it going. That is where the problem lies." But unlike Hockenberry, Bennet does not see this as a new hurdle brought on by a more market-driven environment. "This place has never had a surplus of resources," he says. "There's always been a problem carrying [new programs] forward."

There is some evidence that the old system, which sold programs to stations in package deals rather than individually, provided a cushion for public-service-oriented shows that never could have survived financially on their own. For example, "Enfoque Nacional," a Spanish-language news and feature program that seemed to fit right in line with NPR's desire to broaden its audience, fell under the ax when it could no longer piggyback on the news package that contained "All Things Considered" and "Morning Edition."

José McMurray, former executive producer for the show, accuses NPR of just giving lip service to reaching out to minorities, ethnic groups, the elderly, and children. "Public radio is this beast that is very comfortable with what it has," he says. "It has this niche, which is college graduates, yuppies, and commuters. White liberals sit around over there and say, 'Don't tell me how to be a liberal,' then let programs like 'Enfoque Nacional' die."

Some worthy programming hasn't survived the economic effects of "unbundling" the cultural package. Isabel Ilegria (right) was associate producer with "Enfoque Nacional," a victim of the change. But other magazine and performance programs have continued: "Performance Today" with Martin Goldsmith, The St. Louis Symphony with Leonard Slatkin, and "Weekend Edition" on Sunday with Liane Hansen (top to bottom, opposite).

Doug Bennet did pull together an eclectic study group in 1990, which included people like Sokoni Karanja, who runs a relief agency on the South Side of Chicago. They issued a strategic plan for the network's future that cited broad-based cultural programming as the "key to radio renewal." NPR must cater to the growing elderly population, to children, to minority and ethnic groups like Hispanics, blacks, and Asians, they argued, or it will become obsolete. The question remains, however, whether the network can win over skittish station managers, who are more interested in building a broad-based audience than serving select niches within a market.

The gap between what NPR hopes to do and what it actually does in cultural programming has some people wondering aloud if the department's even worth what little money it does get. Jack Mitchell, a former director of news and information programming who scrounged together $300,000 in 1984 to keep NPR's arts division breathing, believes "cultural programming is a totally ineffective sideshow. In retrospect I think it was a mistake [to give it money]. What has come since has not been worth it."

Struggling editors from the news side, like Cadi Simon from the foreign desk, can't figure out why NPR continues to funnel scarce resources into meager cultural offerings. Outside of the classical music magazine "Performance Today," NPR's cultural department actually produces very little. "As a news person I still don't get it," says Simon. "If most people listen to us and most of the money the stations raise is around us, and most of the reputation comes from what we do, then why don't we get more money? At some point NPR needs to pour it all into the main programs and make them as strong as it can."

Fund-raisers centered around broadcasts of "All Things Considered" and "Morning Edition" do bring in the most money for local stations, but the financial picture is a bit more complicated than that. Cultural programming actually gets a lot of its cash from corporations that issue earmarked grants for certain topics, like jazz or classical music. A dollar earmarked for opera would not necessarily fall into the coffers of the news department if NPR suddenly decided to can its cultural division.

Richard Salant, a former president of CBS News, actually resigned from NPR's board in 1990 to protest the fact that the news division also relies on earmarked grants that target topics like environmental reporting or women's issues. Salant felt such criteria could influence what NPR chose to cover, but the network has not changed its policy.

"Taking the money expands our coverage and gives us greater latitude," Bennet told the *Washington Journalism Review* at the time. "Professionals in the field think we're one of the highest-rated news sources in terms of credibility. The proof is in the pudding."

The answer to more effective funding and fuller programming on both sides may lie in the network coming full circle. Pennekamp agrees that "All Things

Considered" and "Morning Edition" "sacrificed the richer stories" in their quest to become a primary news source, but adds that NPR is "not happy about this. We're actually trying to raise money to establish a cultural desk in the news department. It would provide a focal point for ideas." From 1990 to 1992, Pennekamp's department managed to raise $400,000 in grants for cultural programming in *news*.

Everything has become much more fluid, and Bill Buzenberg welcomes the change. "One reason why we want to start a cultural desk—which would be just like a foreign desk or domestic desk—is because we want to be sure they [cultural stories] stay in," he says.

News already oversees the production of the thirty-minute weekly public affairs program "Horizons," hosted by Vertamae Grosvenor. It searches the "part of America that you've never heard of before," she says, which may bring her to the doorsteps of grandmothers taking care of grandkids left unattended by drug-addicted parents or to the Library of Congress for taped conversations with blacks who worked on Southern plantations before the Civil War.

When NPR put together a tape of highlights to mark its twentieth anniversary in 1990, it included a story by Grosvenor on the history of slave cooking that explored the connection between food and culture. In her melodious, story-teller's voice, she recounted how "in the land of the magnolias, the Africans hungered for the babar and other foods of their homeland like the Israelites in the wilderness longed for food they had known in Egypt. . . . Who knows why the okra made the young bride sad?"

The news department also helped produce "Radio Expeditions: The Unheard World," a special series on natural sounds done in conjunction with National Geographic. The first segment aired during the United Nations' environmental summit in Brazil in June 1992. The special explored the legacy of natural sounds that humans have heard over the millennia: a baby listening to its mother's heart while in the womb; cavemen being lulled "to sleep by pretty much the same night that we can find in the wild today."

Later in the program, Alex Chadwick, who cohosted the program with Lynn Neary, reported on a scientist working in the Bolivian rain forest who tracks hundreds of species of birds solely on the basis of their songs. He rarely sees them, because the canopy is too thick; so he tapes their calls, plays them back, and listens for an answer. Fewer and fewer birds respond now, as they disappear along with their endangered habitat. The scientist's taped recordings must then serve as an archive or echo for a world of sound gone silent.

"Who knows why the okra made the young bride sad?" Vertamae Grosvenor (opposite), host, story teller, and mellifluous presence on "Horizons," leads listeners to unexplored corners of our world, raising and sometimes answering questions like that.

If the news department could maintain its position as a primary news source and add this kind of quality cultural programming to existing news programs, then NPR would have finally arrived where Jack Mitchell—and others—felt it belonged all along.

"It's been a long-term quest for balance," he says. "I've always believed that NPR should end up with current affairs and human affairs, not news and cultural. It should do a magazine program that's half and half. The cultural needs

to be pulled back into the ongoing stream of a magazine like 'All Things Considered.'"

The hard news part of the program would protect the soft features, because stations that needed the headlines would also have to accept the more experimental material. "ATC" has thought about extending its airtime from ninety minutes to two hours, which would provide more space for profiles, mini-documentaries, and issue-oriented discussions. But the member stations have made it clear that they prefer the modular format of "Morning Edition," which makes the prospect of a breezier, lengthier "ATC" rather farfetched.

"Any changes they can make in the news programs that make it easier to break in for station identification or for fund-raising is a good thing," says Gerry Weston, manager of WFPL in Louisville. "I think 'Morning Edition' is a perfectly constructed program. 'ATC' has always been a little slow to change. It reminds me of some old Yankee trader who takes the same approach for 150 years."

"I think every station would like more opportunities in 'All Things Considered,'" says Scott Borden, manager of WNYC-FM in New York City. "Sooner or later NPR is going to have to give in on that one."

But if the network gives in to the stations on format, how can it stand up to them on content? How can it build audience by becoming more user-friendly *and* diversify its programming through narrowcasting when one step seems to cut off the other?

"I hope that people will look back ten years from now and look at the strategic plan that we did in 1990 as the beginning of a whole new institution," says Doug Bennet. The fate of cultural programming will serve as a kind of litmus test for that vision: Will it mingle with news, stand alone with renewed glory, or fade away like an old soldier?

CHAPTER TEN

Curtain Call

For many NPR fans the network remains the sum of its personalities, not an institution. Bob Edwards *is* "Morning Edition," just as Scott Simon *was* "Weekend Edition." Some people think, divorced from their hosts, the programs have no spirit, no life. Listeners who sustain this more intimate connection would never be satisfied with a portrait of the network that didn't include a curtain call for the stars. They want to know how early Edwards gets up in the morning, if Simon is still single, and whether Susan Stamberg's twang comes from a childhood spent in Boston or New York.

Edwards wakes up at 1:30 a.m. every weekday and doesn't like it. He's placed his alarm clock across the room from his bed, which forces him to clear the covers even on the coldest of mornings. After coffee and cereal, he commutes from Arlington, Virginia, down I–66, dodging drunk drivers in his brown Volvo. In 1981, another Volvo he owned, "still running on the dealer's tank of gas," got totaled by a sloshed nineteen-year-old girl. Most days he makes it safely to his office on M Street in downtown Washington by 2:20 a.m, leaves by noon, and has his youngest daughter tuck him in each night by seven. Not the sort of life he envisioned for himself while a business major in the night school at the University of Louisville in the 1960s.

He worked days and took classes at night so he wouldn't become "cannon fodder on the front lines" once he got drafted. "My whole way of going to school as an undergrad was determined by the [Vietnam] war," he says. "It really messed me up. I had to get the degree. It was a lifesaver—literally." He tried to get into the Indiana National Guard, but there weren't any openings. So after a brief stint as a radio announcer for WHEL in New Albany, Indiana, Edwards found himself facing a panel of military screeners who would determine where he'd be stationed.

"I knew this was no time to be shy. I had to go in there and tell them I was Walter Cronkite," he says. "If they didn't put me in broadcasting, boy, they were making a mistake. And I had my FCC license, which really impressed them. They wrote the number down.

"It worked. I didn't even go to school. They put me right into a job doing training tapes for a year. Then I did Korea for a year. I was incredibly lucky. I'm in Korea doing tapes, and there's a war going on." He later anchored the army's six o'clock television news program in Seoul.

When he got out of the military he headed to American University's

"Radio was something I could do," says Noah Adams, who began as a rock-and-roll deejay and moved on to NPR as a writer and tape editor and then "ATC" anchor beginning in 1982.

journalism school, where he met Ed Bliss and really fell for radio. A black-and-white photo of Edwards and his AU classmates hangs in the host's office. They all look so mod, so seventies, so young.

His blondish hair is shorter than it was when that picture was taken, and he's put on twenty-five pounds—a gain he attributes more to his recent decision to quit smoking than to his middle-age metabolism. The added weight on his 6-foot-4-inch frame, his big voice, and a large grin give him a soft, almost cartoon quality. He'd make an easy target for a caricaturist.

Edwards's counterpart on "All Things Considered," Noah Adams, also sprang from Kentucky and says he wound up in radio because "no one in print was offering me a job, and radio was something I could do."

He started out spinning rock-and-roll records as a deejay for a station in Ohio but dropped out of radio to work odd jobs like selling cars, writing ads, and working construction. He tried college and journalism school but pulled out of both. A quiet man given to monosyllable answers when questioned, Adams has little to say about his restless years or why he settled back into radio at WBKY in Lexington, Kentucky, at the age of thirty-two. A few years later he

Bob Edwards arrived at journalism school with more than an abstract interest in broadcasting. His experience — on commercial stations and in the military — made him an old hand among his classmates, including David Molpus (at his right), at American University.

headed for NPR, where he worked as a writer and tape editor. His voice carried him into the anchor seat of "All Things Considered" by 1982 and into the memory banks of millions of NPR listeners. He could probably cash a check in Iowa based on voice identification alone.

His former partner on "All Things Considered," Robert Siegel, has the gift of gab that Adams lacks. Like a tenured college professor, with a greying beard and bald head, Siegel presides over meetings and the newsroom, flashing his sardonic wit.

He first got involved in radio as a student at Columbia University in New York. He commuted to school and wanted a way to break into campus life. Unlike the land-grant universities in the Midwest, Columbia did not use the airwaves to serve the larger community. "The radio station was the equivalent of an undergrad newspaper, except that it was licensed to the university," says Siegel. The AM station basically fed music to the dormitories, while the slightly stronger FM station provided news and other programming for the larger campus.

"I enjoyed it a lot," he says. "I liked rock-and-roll music, so I did an oldies radio show that nobody could hear [because the signal was too weak]. Each year I became increasingly more interested in the possibilities." By the time of the Columbia student riot in 1968, Siegel had become completely enamored of radio. "I was bitten," he says.

The student protest centered around the university's decision to build a new gym on public land in Morningside Park, a move that threatened to irritate the already strained relations Columbia had with the Harlem community. The protesters also objected to the school's participation in the Institute for Defense Analysis, which performed research for the Defense Department. Such policies, they said, were evidence of racism and complicity with warmongers. They staged a sit-in at the proposed site for the gym, then moved onto the campus, where they took over Hamilton Hall and, later, four other Columbia buildings. A dean and two other administrators got trapped inside for hours. City police, armed with heavy boots and night sticks, beat their way in, which lead to an all-out riot. The demonstration marked the beginning of more militant antiwar protests on college campuses across the country.

Siegel anchored the university's radio broadcasts around-the-clock during the uproar. After all his experience in radio, as an overseas correspondent in London, Eastern Europe, and the Middle East, after all the hot battles in NPR's newsroom as news director or senior editor or host, Siegel still ranks those college-day newscasts as among the most thrilling of his life. They helped push him into a radio career, first at a small commercial station in Long Island, then, after nearly a year of unemployment, to the Riverside Church station, WRVR, in New York. Like Adams and Scott Simon, he tried journalism school, but found the textbook approach to his profession unappealing and dropped out.

Since his arrival at NPR in the early 1970s, he's held nearly every key post in the network's news division. He's been instrumental in the network's push to become a primary news source, something he considers essential for a more "mature NPR."

Such thoughts put Siegel right in line with the three powerful women correspondents—Linda Wertheimer, Cokie Roberts, and Nina Totenberg—known variously as the "Fallopian Trio," the "Troika," or by other less savory nicknames.

> What we did was to come as an entire generation and break down the obstacles, and we all have wounds to show for it. We all have splinters. We had people tell us all along the way that we weren't qualified to deliver the news, that we weren't authoritative enough. We would have meetings with men in high positions and find their hands on our knees. We would have invitations from those people to hotel rooms. All kinds of propositions. —*Cokie Roberts, special correspondent*

Practically every major story written about the network seems to center on "The Women of NPR." People claim they influence key hiring decisions and determine which stories get on the air. Some stations managers call them "sanctimonious and arrogant," others consider them the backbone of the news operation.

"Everyone knows where the real power is, and those are women," Bob Edwards says with a laugh. "When it comes time to renegotiate a contract, those are good people to have on your side.

"Their journalistic instincts are just impeccable," he adds, "so it's great to let them lead the way."

The very fact that reporters still single out NPR because it has so many women in top jobs underscores the sexist nature of journalism and society in

general. If the three most powerful correspondents at the network were men, there wouldn't be any story. Such inconsistencies have convinced the members of the Troika that whatever gains they may have made aren't enough. Newcomers still need to battle bias as aggressively as their predecessors did.

Wertheimer had to go overseas to the BBC in London to get her first radio job when she got out of Wellesley in 1965. When she returned to the states she became the first woman hired by WCBS in New York for a nonclerical position. She turned to radio, in part, because she knew that a "flat-chested, brainy, dark" woman who wears no watch, carries no purse, and rarely puts on makeup would never make it in television. When NPR hired her as a correspondent in 1971, she quickly moved to the political beat, which placed her in the

Linda Wertheimer turned to radio, she says, because she knew that a "flat-chested, brainy, dark" woman who wears no watch, carries no purse, and rarely puts on makeup would never make it on television.

middle of four presidential campaigns, the Panama Canal Treaty debates, and hearings for Watergate and Iran-contra. Actually, former NPR President Frank Mankiewicz took a calculated risk when he assigned Wertheimer to the key Panama Canal story. It marked the first time *any* broadcast network had been allowed to cover a Senate debate live. The stations grumbled when Mankiewicz handed the hot seat to a woman. But he had felt her fire his very first week on the job. Just after the board elected him president in 1977, a woman in a jumpsuit came up to him and said, "Hi, I'm Linda Wertheimer. I'm your shop steward, and we're striking you next Friday." Mankiewicz eventually sat down with the staff and hammered out a new contract, but he always remembered that it was Wertheimer—a woman—who spearheaded the employees' attack.

She grew up in Carlsbad, New Mexico, where such assertiveness hardly qualified as a redeeming quality but did help explain why a teenage girl seemed set on a career in a field like journalism. When Wertheimer brought her mother along on an assignment on Capitol Hill one day, she "thought [her mother would] be impressed by the fact that members of Congress called me by my first name, that I could call senators off the floor and ask them questions, that I was very aggressive about getting what I wanted," Wertheimer said in a *Lear's* magazine interview. "But at the end of the day, she turned to me and said, 'I didn't bring you up to talk to people like that.'"

Wertheimer can indulge in a much softer approach to her work as a host of "All Things Considered," a spot she secured in 1989 after Noah Adams left to launch his ill-fated variety show, "Good Evening," in Minnesota. The three-host rotation on "All Things Considered" made it possible for her to still hit the trail for the 1992 presidential campaign. Her marriage to Fred Wertheimer, president of the citizens' lobbying organization Common Cause, will keep her in touch with the Washington game even if she elects to pull out of political reporting altogether.

Throughout her NPR career, Wertheimer often teamed with congressional correspondent Cokie Roberts, whom she first knew as a fellow student at Wellesley College. After living overseas with her husband, who was then a reporter for *The New York Times* and is now an editor at *U.S. News and World Report,* and having two children, Roberts returned to the states looking for a job. She'd done a few stand-up items for CBS News in Athens and at one point had worked on a children's television program, "Serendipity"; but her broadcast experience remained sketchy at best. When Wertheimer told her about a job at the fledgling public radio network, Roberts applied and got hired to cover

The daughter of two members of the House of Representatives, Cokie Roberts resisted covering the Congress. She concludes, as others have, "As it turns out, I was good at it."

family and lifestyle issues. "I never intended to do this work," she says. "We are ladies of a certain age and weren't expected to do any work."

"What we did was to come as an entire generation and break down the obstacles, and we all have wounds to show for it. We all have splinters," she told a reporter for the *Los Angeles Times Sunday Magazine*. "We had people tell us all along the way that we weren't qualified to deliver the news, that we weren't authoritative enough. We would have meetings with men in high positions and find their hands on our knees. We would have invitations from those people to hotel rooms. All kinds of propositions."

She not only had to face external pressures, but also pressures from within. As the daughter of Rep. Hale Boggs, a Democrat from New Orleans who probably would have been Speaker of the House if he hadn't died in a plane crash over Alaska in 1972, and Lindy Boggs, who succeeded her husband and went on to serve in the House for nearly twenty years, Roberts says the last thing she wanted to do was cover Congress. But when the network switched her to that beat, she found that her lifelong exposure to the Capitol Hill culture gave her an inside advantage as a journalist. "As it turns out, I was good at it," she notes with a laugh.

As her star rose within the media establishment, Roberts began to branch out, making contributions to "The MacNeil/Lehrer NewsHour," "Washington Week in Review," "This Week with David Brinkley," and Ted Koppel's "Nightline." In 1988 she signed on as a correspondent for ABC News. "There's no way you can afford to work just for NPR," she notes. But she remains committed to the radio network that took a chance on her during her salad days, and she still provides daily reports for "Morning Edition." When asked how she developed her polished, deep-throated broadcast persona, she responds with a laugh, "Oh, my voice sounds exactly like my mother's."

Such off-hand remarks and witticisms help shield Roberts from being stereotyped as a bitch just because she's an aggressive, successful woman. Her fellow Troika member Nina Totenberg has had no such luck.

Totenberg flashed her trademark edge early in her career as a print reporter for the now defunct *National Observer*. She penned an aggressive profile of then-FBI director J. Edgar Hoover, who shot back a letter to the editor demanding that she be fired. The paper published Hoover's response instead. Later, as a reporter at the sassy magazine *New Times*, Totenberg wrote an article on "The 10 Dumbest Members of Congress" that people still refer to and imitate. By the time she rolled into NPR in 1975 as a legal affairs correspondent, she'd already established herself as a go-for-the-throat kind of journalist.

But her long string of scoops and tough-nosed approach didn't stop the rumors when she started cracking the byzantine world at the U.S. Supreme Court, probably the most closed-door organization in Washington. Male reporters on the beat accused her of having an affair with Justice Potter Stewart. How else, they claimed, could she consistently get insider information?

J. Edgar Hoover once tried to get Nina Totenberg fired, Sen. Alan Simpson once raged at her, but the head of Harvard's Nieman program says, "She is one of the most knowledgeable . . . reporters in the business . . ."

132

CHARLES EVANS HUGHES
ELEVENTH CHIEF JUSTICE
1930~1941

133

Susan Stamberg says her job at NPR resulted more from NPR's lousy salaries than anything else. "We were here for all the wrong reasons, but in the end it was a good thing that we were here."

"It's astounding to me how Nina becomes a lightning rod for other journalists," Bill Kovach, former *New York Times* reporter and Washington bureau chief and current curator for Harvard University's Nieman Foundation, told *Lear's* magazine. "She is one of the most knowledgeable and aggressive reporters in the business; but whenever she breaks a story, the first reaction of the Washington press corps is 'What do you want? She's sleeping with a justice or someone else.' No one says those things about any male reporter, some of whom wouldn't think twice about sleeping with someone to get a story."

Totenberg, who has consistently refuted such charges, does occasionally socialize with several of the justices and their wives and knows most of the staffers at the Supreme Court on a first-name basis. Such familiarity leads to colorful insights, like what the Brethren thought of Justice Clarence Thomas's decision to appear on the cover of *People* magazine after his grueling confirmation process. "He didn't do himself any favors with the court," she says. "All was not happy in Mudville."

She stays with NPR, despite the low salaries and her increased fame, "because it doesn't act like it owns me," she says, "and lets me do work that I respect." Like Roberts, she's appeared regularly on "Nightline" and "The MacNeil/Lehrer NewsHour," though she recently dropped out of MacNeil/Lehrer to take up duties as a special correspondent for NBC.

The Troika opened gates for women broadcasters, stirring up a lot of venom from fellow professionals as they went; but in many ways they just widened a hole first made by former "ATC" host Susan Stamberg. As Robert Siegel pointed out in an interview with the *Los Angeles Times*, "once she established her presence on the air, it became unthinkable to have a broadcast with all male voices."

Of course Stamberg didn't just hop into the host's chair that made her the first woman to anchor a nightly national newscast in America. When she graduated from Barnard College with a degree in English and sociology, she figured she had three choices: to teach, to marry, or to work in publishing. She chose the third option and got a job as an editorial assistant for *Daedalus*, the journal for the American Academy of Arts and Sciences. While there she met her husband, Lou, who worked with the State Department. She followed him to Washington, D.C., where she took on a low-level editorial job at *The New Republic*. Bored with working as an office gofer, she jumped at the opportunity to venture into radio as a producer and host of a local nightly newsmagazine at WAMU at American University.

Stamberg had the opportunity to really learn radio as a host, producer, program director, and manager before she left WAMU to go to India with her husband. When she returned to the states in the late 1960s, she stayed at home with her infant son for nearly two years before reentering the work force. By 1971, she was ready for a job with limited hours, so she took a part-time tape editing position at NPR. She floated there for a few months until the day "All Things Considered" host Mike Waters went on vacation, and Bill Siemering

Robert Siegel has experience about as broad as one can have at NPR: overseas correspondent, senior editor, news director, and host of several shows. The enthusiasm for radio that first led him to it remains as strong as ever.

asked Stamberg to sit in. Somehow the voice that hailed from Newark, New Jersey, that got its New York edge at the Big Apple's High School of Music and Arts, and that came with an effusive personality that even the darkest news couldn't dampen, just fit the program.

They signed her up even though she could only work part-time. They let her tape most of her material before she went on the air and let her go home by five-thirty every night, even though "ATC" didn't end until six. "They really made adjustments for me," she says. "I'm not even sure that you'd see that today, though NPR is still light-years ahead of most places in terms of numbers of women in powerful positions. I was the first on the air. I opened doors. I had to work very hard. You know that women always work ten times harder," but NPR was sensitive to the other demands on her, or, in her terms, "receptive" to her needs as a wife and mother of a young child.

She still has mixed feelings about her early successes, because they resulted more from NPR's lousy salaries than anything else. The network's pay scale discouraged talented men, which left the door ajar for women to fill prime reporting spots that they never could have secured anywhere else. "We were married, and that was before everyone had to have a two-income family," Stamberg says, "so our husbands could supplement. It was *wrong*. We were here for all the wrong reasons, but in the end it was a good thing that we were here."

Today no one even blinks when someone like Lynn Neary takes over Robert Siegel's job as a host for "All Things Considered." After eight years of anchoring "Weekend All Things Considered," she has the experience and voice recognition necessary for such a high-profile position. Her gender has become irrelevant.

Though she's around the same age as Totenberg, Neary doesn't talk much about the sexism she faced coming up through the ranks. Instead she highlights her own indecision. As a Fordham University graduate in 1971, she wanted to become a journalist, but it "seemed so out of my reach. I was afraid of it," she says seriously.

She tried working at a psychiatric hospital, because she thought she might like social work, then in a law office, and finally, acting. "Hey, remember, it was the seventies." She laughs. By the end of the decade she decided to go back to her first idea—journalism—because it seemed to be the only profession where she could be both socially responsible and creative.

"So I moved out of New York and to a small commercial radio station in Rocky Mount, North Carolina," she says. "That was a big shift, let me tell you, but I knew within a week that I had made the right decision." Someone there told her she'd be ideal for public radio, so she began scouting for jobs across the country and wound up at WOSU in Columbus, Ohio. She honed her basic reporting skills there covering "police department things," then secured a job at NPR's headquarters as a writer and announcer for the newscaster unit of "Morning Edition."

In 1989 she was chosen to fill one of the vacant seats on the weekday "All Things Considered," only to have the offer pulled at the last minute. Linda Wertheimer took the slot instead, and Neary remained on the weekend program.

The mix-up raised quite a stir at the time. When a *Washington Post* reporter questioned Adam Powell about it, he barked, "There is no job offer until it's final."

Doug Bennet took a somewhat more chagrined approach. "We did not handle that situation well. I don't think people should have been misled."

The network continued to play cat and mouse with Neary even after it gave her Siegel's spot on "ATC" in the summer of 1992. Management called it a "temporary" arrangement that would only hold until after the presidential election. Then, well, who knows? Afraid to make waves as she sat between her old and new job, Neary refused to comment on the situation. She did acknowledge that she enjoys the more leisurely pace of the weekend program, which "definitely has more texture and feel and is less driven by news. A part of me just wants to go back to 'Weekend ATC.'" But when pressed to say if she'd stay on the weekday magazine if given the chance, she said nothing.

Neary could thank John Hockenberry for her predicament, since his departure for ABC started the musical chairs. Someone had to fill his spot as host on the call-in program "Talk of the Nation."

The self-described wiseass may have left NPR, but no portrait of the network would be complete without him. He got his first major airtime on the network as a freelancer covering the 1980 eruption of Mount St. Helens. Chris Koch, who was the producer of "All Things Considered" at the time, remembers this young guy sending in "incredible stuff. He was heading up every news hour." Then one day, for some inexplicable reason, Hockenberry didn't call in his piece, even though he knew it was slated to lead the show. Four-thirty. Nothing. Four-forty-five. Nothing. "I had this four-and-a-half minute hole at

Lynn Neary, though wanting to be a journalist, took a circuitous route after college to NPR, trying the fringes of social work, the law, and the theater first. At NPR, she traveled from writer to newscaster to host on "ATC" in the summer of 1992. She's not done yet.

the top of the newscast," says Koch. "I had to push the whole lineup forward and hope he came through later.

"At five-fifteen he calls and I'm totally berserk. 'Why didn't you call?' I screamed. He said he couldn't get to a phone. 'Just use a god damn phone booth!' 'I couldn't get the wheelchair in the door,' Hockenberry tells me. Wow. We had no idea that he was working out of a wheelchair. I was just stunned. 'Yeah,' he told me, 'I'm paralyzed from the waist down.' My respect for the guy just skyrocketed."

Not long after the Mount St. Helens episode, NPR hired Hockenberry as a full-time correspondent based in Washington, D.C., where he immediately found himself confronted with the task of establishing his credibility while "butt-level" to the rest of the staff. He quickly developed a reputation for being somewhat cantankerous.

After a few years of reporting for "ATC," Hockenberry became restless and applied for and got a Benton Fellowship at the University of Chicago. He headed for the Windy City and worked off-and-on for a year as NPR's Midwest correspondent. During all this time he persisted in "petitioning for a foreign assignment." A man in a wheelchair traveling through the sands of the Middle East or down the streets of Beijing? Forget it. He couldn't even get a hearing.

But all that changed when he applied for a spot in NASA's "Journalists in Space" program. "In a weightless environment, the last thing you need is your legs," he rationalized at the time. Besides, he'd been doing wheelchair marathons and was in top condition. He made the last cut and wound up on CBS's morning news show along with fellow finalist Walter Cronkite.

"John, I understand you want to be the first paraplegic in space," said Forrest Sawyer.

"No, Forrest, I want to be the first *journalist* in space," he responded.

The whole issue became moot when the space shuttle *Challenger* exploded in 1986 and NASA had to cancel the program. Back at NPR, however, Hockenberry's success in the application process placed him in a new light among management. Soon after the CBS broadcast, Adam Powell offered Hockenberry a post in the Middle East.

It became apparent that management hadn't completely thought through its decision to station Hockenberry in Jerusalem when it refused to pay his taxi bills. Without the cabs he had no way of getting around to his assignments. They gave in after Hockenberry convinced them that they were just setting him up for failure if they cut off additional resources for his transportation.

During his three years in the Middle East, Hockenberry talked PLO thugs into carrying him up the stairs for a personal interview with Yassar Arafat; he almost got trampled to death as he wheeled through the rioting mob at the Ayatollah Khomeini's funeral; and he learned all the tricks that made his Gulf War coverage from Israel so distinctive.

When he returned to the states, he plunged into work on "Heat." When that failed, he turned to "Talk of the Nation." Even when he hosted out of

Washington, D.C., he lived in New York City. He'd stay in a hotel in the capital four nights a week, then return home to his Upper East Side apartment on the weekends.

Hockenberry's successes and incredible sense of humor make it easy sometimes to forget about his wheelchair. But at one point in an interview for a small newspaper, Hockenberry commented that the wheels of his chair leave "their signature in rolling patterns on everything I do and everything I am. And it is a good thing—this duet of human beings and wheels. It teaches you things."

His fellow journalists have learned enough to focus on his work rather than his handicap. When ABC hired him away from NPR, Hockenberry became the first wheelchair-bound correspondent on network television.

Despite all the harsh complaints he's levied at public radio in recent years, Hockenberry made it clear when he left NPR that the radio network remains a place he loves and admires. He thanked it for "being right there behind me—as much as a nonprofit, budget-weary company can be. There's no other organization that would have sent me to the Middle East. None."

NPR lost another of its trademark characters in the summer of 1992—Scott Simon, who went to NBC-TV to host the new Saturday morning "Today" show. Simon's interest in radio ran in the family—his father was a comedian and radio personality; but when Simon went to college to study journalism, he—like so many of his NPR colleagues—found the trade school approach to the profession distasteful, so he dropped out. A native of Chicago, Simon got his start with NPR in that city, first as a freelancer and later as bureau chief.

His home town took to its dark-haired, dark-eyed golden boy immediately, showering him with praise in the local press for his work at NPR and with letters from women infatuated with his sensitive voice and style. "Someone once said if the world were ending, she'd like Susan Stamberg to announce it," a columnist wrote in the *Chicago Sun-Times Sunday Magazine* in 1989. "As for you,

Asked if he wanted to be the first paraplegic in space, John Hockenberry replied, "No, I want to be the first journalist in space."

you'd take Simon. He'd be comforting, cogent, lucid, perceptive, sad, telling you that life and the struggles of civilization hadn't been for naught."

Robert Siegel once called Simon's "Weekend Edition" a show about "the moral life of America," a characterization that closely matches Simon's off-mike persona. A practicing Quaker, teetotaler, devoted pacifist, alleged vegetarian, and basically an all-around straight guy with the wide soft eyes of a social worker, Simon has made his work his life. In several interviews he has commented on how his career cuts into his personal life; but he keeps going and keeps single—much to the delight of man-hungry women listeners who consistently offer to be his escort if he should happen to visit the public radio station in their town.

When he left "Weekend Edition," Simon bade farewell with his usual tear-jerker flair: "Over the past fifteen years it has been my privilege, and I do believe a blessing, to have been a part of a group of people who have created one of the most cherished institutions of American life. For millions of Americans, the initials N-P-R have come to symbolize civility and conviction. . . ."

For countless NPR employees, public radio has represented a haven from many of the crass trends in media. They can do stories measured in minutes, not

seconds. They can do profiles of offbeat Americans in no-name places and still call it news. They can push and tug and improvise, a professional indulgence that helps offset the cost of working for such paltry salaries.

"There's almost an ethical problem about getting people to work for the salaries we pay them," says Doug Bennet. Starting reporters earn around $20,000, star correspondents might top $60,000, and big-name hosts get a whopping $80,000, which is about how much the television networks allot for news anchors' wardrobes. "It's not something I feel particularly comfortable about," he adds. "I mean, Bob [Edwards] is in that goddamn studio every day at two o'clock in the morning, and he has kids. You can compensate to some degree by having an organization that's well-regarded and compensate with intellectual returns to some degree, and it works. But from a management point of view, I don't think we do as much for our employees as we ought."

Some stars, like Hockenberry and Simon, do break away, but even when they go they always seem to look back. They move to a new job but call it a "sabbatical." They try television but somehow still prefer talking about the wonders and potential of radio. Few NPR employees ever completely cut the threads that bind them to the unique world of public broadcasting.

A new generation of top-notch reporters and hosts who happen to be women has arrived at NPR: political correspondents Elizabeth Arnold, Renee Montagne, and Mara Liasson (left to right).

NPR Member Stations

ALABAMA

Birmingham	WBHM(FM)	90.3
Dothan	WRWA(FM)†	88.7
Huntsville	WLRH(FM)	89.3
Jacksonville	WLJS(FM)*	91.9
Montgomery/Troy	WTSU(FM)	89.9
Muscle Shoals	WQPR(FM)†	88.7
Tuscaloosa	WUAL(FM)	91.5

ALASKA

Anchorage	KSKA(FM)	91.1
Fairbanks	KUAC(FM)	104.7
Galena	KIYU(AM)†	910
Haines	KHNS(FM)	102.3
Homer	KBBI(AM)	890
Juneau	KTOO(FM)	104.3
Kenai	KCZP(FM)†	91.9
Ketchikan	KRBD(FM)	105.9
Kodiak	KMXT(FM)	100.1
Petersburg	KFSK(FM)	100.9
Sand Point	KSDP(AM)†	840
Sitka	KCAW(FM)	104.7
Talkeetna	KTNA(FM)†	88.5
Valdez	KCHU(AM)	770

ARIZONA

Flagstaff	KNAU(FM)	88.7
Phoenix	KJZZ(FM)	91.5
Tuba City	KGHR(FM)†	91.5
Tucson	KUAT(AM)	1550
Yuma	KAWC(AM)	1320
	KAWC(FM)†	88.9

ARKANSAS

El Dorado	KBSA(FM)†	90.9
Fayetteville	KUAF(FM)	91.3
Jonesboro	KASU(FM)	91.9
Little Rock	KLRE(FM)†	90.5
	KUAR(FM)	89.1

CALIFORNIA

Arcata	KHSU(FM)	90.5
Bakersfield	KPRX(FM)†	89.1
Burney	KNCA(FM)†	89.7
Chico	KCHO(FM)	91.7
Fresno	KVPR(FM)	89.3
	KUBO(FM)*	88.7
Groveland	KXSR(FM)†	91.7
Pasadena	KPCC(FM)	89.3
Philo	KZYX(FM)	90.7
Sacramento	KXPR(FM)	90.9
	KXJZ(FM)†	88.9
San Bernardino	KVCR(FM)	91.9
San Diego	KPBS(FM)	89.5
San Francisco	KALW(FM)	91.7
	KQED(FM)	88.5
San Luis Obispo	KCBX(FM)	90.1
San Mateo	KCSM(FM)	91.1
Santa Cruz	KUSP(FM)	88.9
Santa Monica	KCRW(FM)	89.9
Stockton	KUOP(FM)	91.3

COLORADO

Alamosa	KRZA(FM)*	88.7
Aspen	KAJX(FM)*	91.5
Boulder	KGNU(FM)	88.5
Carbondale	KDNK(FM)*	90.5
Colorado Springs	KRCC(FM)	91.5
Denver	KCFR(FM)	90.1
	KUVO(FM)	89.3
Grand Junction	KPRN(FM)†	89.5
Greeley	KUNC(FM)	91.5
Ignacio	KSUT(FM)	91.3
Paonia	KVNF(FM)*	90.9
Telluride	KOTO(FM)*	91.7

CONNECTICUT

Fairfield	WSHU(FM)	91.1
Hartford	WPKT(FM)	90.5
Norwich	WNPR(FM)†	89.1
Stamford	WEDW (FM)†	88.5
Willimantic	WECS(FM)†	90.1

DISTRICT OF COLUMBIA

	WAMU(FM)	88.5
	WDCU(FM)	90.1
	WETA(FM)	90.9

FLORIDA

Ft. Myers	WSFP(FM)	90.1
Ft. Pierce	WQCS(FM)	88.9
Gainesville	WUFT(FM)	89.1

†Associate Station   *Auxiliary Station

FLORIDA (Continued)

Jacksonville	WJCT(FM)	89.9
Miami	WLRN(FM)	91.3
Orlando	WMFE(FM)	90.7
Panama City	WKGC(FM)	90.7
	WKGC(AM)†	1480
Pensacola	WUWF(FM)	88.1
Tallahassee	WFSU(FM)	88.9
	WFSQ(FM)†	91.5
Tampa	WUSF(FM)	89.7
West Palm Beach	WXEL(FM)	90.7

GEORGIA

Albany	WUNV(FM)†	91.7
Athens	WUGA(FM)	91.7
Atlanta	WABE(FM)	90.1
	WCLK(FM)	91.9
Augusta	WACG(FM)†	90.7
Columbus	WJSP(FM)	88.1
	WTJB(FM)†	91.7
Macon	WDCO(FM)†	89.7
Savannah	WSVH(FM)	91.1
Tifton	WABR(FM)†	107.5
Valdosta	WWET(FM)†	91.7
Waycross	WXVS(FM)†	90.1

HAWAII

Honolulu	KHPR(FM)	88.1
	KIPO(FM)†	89.3
Pearl City	KIPO(AM)†	1380
Wailuku	KKUA(FM)†	90.7

IDAHO

Boise	KBSU(FM)	90.3
	KBSU(AM)†	730
	KBSX (FM)	91.5
McCall	KBSM(FM)†	91.7
Moscow	KRFA(FM)†	91.7
Rexburg	KRIC(FM)*	100.5
Twin Falls	KBSW(FM)†	91.7

ILLINOIS

Carbondale	WSIU(FM)	91.9
Chicago	WBEZ(FM)	91.5
DeKalb	WNIU(FM)	89.5
Edwardsville	WSIE(FM)	88.7
Macomb	WIUM(FM)	91.3
Normal	WGLT(FM)	89.1
Olney	WUSI(FM)†	90.5
Peoria	WCBU(FM)	89.9
Quincy	WWQC(FM)*	90.3
Rock Island	WVIK(FM)	90.3
Rockford	WNIJ(FM)	90.5
Springfield	WSSU(FM)	91.9
Urbana	WILL(AM)	580
	WILL (FM)	90.9

INDIANA

Bloomington	WFIU(FM)	103.7
Elkhart	WVPE(FM)	88.1
Evansville	WNIN(FM)	88.3
Fort Wayne	WBNI(FM)	89.1
Indianapolis	WFYI(FM)	90.1
	WAJC(FM)	104.5
Muncie	WBST(FM)	92.1
North Manchester	WBKE(FM)†	89.5
Richmond	WVXR(FM)†	89.3

IOWA

Ames	WOI(FM)	90.1
	WOI(AM)	640
Cedar Falls	KUNI(FM)	90.9
Decorah	KLCD(FM)†	89.5
Fort Dodge	KTPR(FM)	91.1
Iowa City	KSUI(FM)	91.7
	WSUI(AM)	910
Mason City	KUNY(FM)†	91.5
Sioux City	KWIT(FM)	90.3
Waterloo	KBBG(FM)	88.1

KANSAS

Great Bend	KHCT(FM)†	90.9
Hill City	KZNA(FM)†	90.5
Hutchinson	KHCC(FM)	90.1
Lawrence	KANU(FM)	91.5
Manhattan	KKSU(AM)	580
Pierceville	KANZ(FM)	91.1
Pittsburg	KRPS(FM)	89.9
Salina	KHCD(FM)†	89.5
Wichita	KMUW(FM)	89.1

KENTUCKY

Bowling Green	WKYU(FM)	88.9
Elizabethtown	WKUE(FM)†	90.9
Hazard	WEKH(FM)†	90.9
Henderson	WKPB(FM)†	89.5
Highland Heights	WNKU(FM)	89.7
Lexington	WUKY(FM)	91.3
Louisville	WFPL(FM)	89.3
Morehead	WMKY(FM)	90.3
Murray	WKMS(FM)	91.3
Richmond	WEKU(FM)	88.9
Somerset	WDCL(FM)†	89.7

LOUISIANA

Alexandria	KLSA(FM)†	90.7
Baton Rouge	WRKF(FM)	89.3
	WBRH(FM)†	90.3
Lafayette	KRVS(FM)	88.7
Monroe	KEDM(FM)	90.3
New Orleans	WWNO(FM)	89.9
Shreveport	KDAQ(FM)	89.9

MAINE

Bangor	WMEH(FM)	90.9
Calais	WMED(FM)†	89.7
Portland	WMEA(FM)	90.1
Presque Isle	WMEM(FM)†	106.1
Waterville	WMEW(FM)†	91.3

MARYLAND

Baltimore	WEAA(FM)	88.9
	WJHU(FM)	88.1
Princess Anne	WESM(FM)	91.3
Salisbury	WSCL(FM)	89.5

MASSACHUSETTS

Amherst	WFCR(FM)	88.5
Boston	WBUR(FM)	90.9
	WGBH(FM)	89.7
Harwich	WCCT(FM)†	90.3
Sandwich	WSDH(FM)†	91.5
Worcester	WICN(FM)	90.5

MICHIGAN

Alpena	WCML(FM)†	91.7
Ann Arbor	WUOM(FM)	91.7
Bay City	WUCX(FM)†	90.1
Detroit	WDET(FM)	101.9
East Jordan	WIZY(FM)†	100.9
East Lansing	WKAR(FM)	90.5
	WKAR(AM)	870
Flint	WFUM(FM)†	91.1
Grand Rapids	WGVU(FM)	88.5
	WGVU(AM)	1480
	WVGR(FM)†	104.1
Houghton	WGGL(FM)†	91.1
Interlochen	WIAA(FM)	88.7
Kalamazoo	WMUK(FM)	102.1
Marquette	WNMU(FM)	90.1
Mt. Pleasant	WCMU(FM)	89.5
Sault Ste. Marie	WCMZ(FM)†	98.3
Twin Lake	WBLV(FM)	90.3
Ypsilanti	WEMU(FM)	89.1

MINNESOTA

Austin	KMSK(FM)†	91.3
Appleton	KRSU(FM)†	91.3
Bemidji	KCRB(FM)†	88.5
Brainerd	KBPR(FM)†	90.7
Buhl	WIRR(FM)†	90.9
Collegeville	KNSR(FM)†	88.9
Duluth/Superior	KUWS(FM)†	91.3
Duluth	WSCN(FM)†	100.5
Grand Rapids	KAXE(FM)	91.7
La Crescent	KXLC(FM)†	91.1
Mankato	KMSU(FM)	89.7
Minneapolis/St. Paul	KNOW(FM)	91.1
Moorhead	KCCD(FM)†	91.1
Northfield	WCAL(FM)	89.3
Rochester	KLSE(FM)	91.7
	KZSE(FM)†	90.7

St. Peter	KNGA(FM)†	91.5
Thief River Falls	KNTN(FM)†	102.7
Worthington	KRSW(FM)	91.7

MISSISSIPPI

Biloxi	WMAH(FM)†	90.3
Bude	WMAU(FM)†	88.9
Booneville	WMAE(FM)†	89.5
Greenwood	WMAO(FM)†	90.9
Jackson	WJSU(FM)	88.5
	WMPN(FM)	91.3
Lorman	WPRL(FM)	91.7
Meridian	WMAW(FM)†	88.1
Mississippi State	WMAB(FM)†	89.9
Oxford	WMAV(FM)†	90.3
Senatobia	WKNA(FM)†	88.9

MISSOURI

Cape Girardeau	KRCU(FM)*	90.9
Columbia	KBIA(FM)	91.3
Kansas City	KCUR(FM)	89.3
Maryville	KXCV(FM)	90.5
Point Lookout	KCOZ(FM)†	90.5
Rolla	KUMR(FM)	88.5
Springfield	KSMU(FM)	91.1
St. Louis	KWMU(FM)	90.7
Warrensburg	KCMW(FM)	90.9

MONTANA

Billings	KEMC(FM)	91.7
Bozman	KBMC(FM)†	102.1
Great Falls	KGPR(FM)†	89.9
Havre	KNMC(FM)†	90.1
Miles City	KECC(FM)†	90.7
Missoula	KUFM(FM)	89.1

NEBRASKA

Alliance	KTNE(FM)†	91.1
Bassett	KMNE(FM)†	90.3
Chadron	KCNE(FM)†	91.9
Hastings	KHNE(FM)†	89.1
Lexington	KLNE(FM)†	88.7
Lincoln	KUCV(FM)	90.9
Merriman	KRNE(FM)†	91.5
Norfolk	KXNE(FM)†	89.3
North Platte	KPNE(FM)†	91.7
Omaha	KIOS(FM)	91.5

NEVADA

Elko	KNCC(FM)†	91.5
Las Vegas	KNPR(FM)	89.5
Panaca	KLNR(FM)†	91.7
Reno	KUNR(FM)	88.7
Tonopah	KTPH(FM)†	91.7

NEW HAMPSHIRE

Concord	WEVO(FM)	89.1

†Associate Station   *Auxiliary Station

NEW MEXICO

Albuquerque	KUNM(FM)	89.9
Gallup	KGLP(FM)†	90.5
Las Cruces	KRWG(FM)	90.7
Maljamar	KMTH(FM)†	98.7
Portales	KENW(FM)	89.5

NEW YORK

Albany	WAMC(FM)	90.3
Alfred	WALF(FM)†	89.7
Binghamton	WSKG(FM)	89.3
Buffalo	WBFO(FM)	88.7
Canajoharie	WCAN(FM)†	93.3
Canton	WSLU(FM)	89.5
Fredonia	WCVF(FM)†	88.7
Geneva	WEOS(FM)*	89.7
Ithaca	WSQG(FM)†	90.9
Jeffersonville	WJFF(FM)*	90.5
Kingston	WAMK(FM)†	90.9
Malone	WSLO(FM)†	90.9
Middletown	WOSR(FM)†	91.7
New York City	WNYC(FM)	93.9
	WNYC(AM)	820
Oneonta	WSQC(FM)†	91.7
Oswego	WRVO(FM)	89.9
Peru	WXLU(FM)†	88.3
Plattsburgh	WCFE(FM)	91.9
Rochester	WXXI(AM)	1370
Saranac Lake	WSLL(FM)†	90.5
Syracuse	WCNY(FM)	91.3
	WAER(FM)	88.3
Ticonderoga	WANC(FM)†	103.9
Utica	WRVN(FM)†	91.9
	WUNY(FM)†	89.5
Watertown	WJNY(FM)†	90.9
	WRVJ (FM)†	91.7

NORTH CAROLINA

Asheville	WCQS(FM)	88.1
Chapel Hill	WUNC(FM)	91.5
Charlotte	WFAE(FM)	90.7
Fayetteville	WFSS(FM)	89.1
Franklin	WFQS(FM)†	91.3
New Bern	WTEB(FM)	89.3
Rocky Mount	WESQ(FM)†	90.9
Spindale	WNCW(FM)	88.7
Wilmington	WHQR(FM)	91.3
Winston-Salem	WFDD(FM)	88.5

NORTH DAKOTA

Belacourt	KEYA(FM)	88.5
Bismarck	KCND(FM)	90.5
Dickinson	KDPR(FM)†	89.9
Fargo	KDSU(FM)	91.9
Grand Forks	KFJM(AM)	1370
	KFJM(FM)	89.3
Minot	KMPR(FM)†	88.9
Williston	KPPR(FM)†	89.5

OHIO

Athens	WOUB(FM)	91.3
	WOUB(AM)	1340
Cambridge	WOUC(FM)†	89.1
Chillicothe	WVXC(FM)†	89.3
	WOUH(FM)†	91.9
Cincinnati	WGUC(FM)	90.9
	WVXU(FM)	91.7
Cleveland	WCPN(FM)	90.3
Columbus	WCBE(FM)	90.5
	WOSU(AM)	820
	WOSU(FM)	89.7
Ironton	WOUL(FM)†	89.1
Kent	WKSU(FM)	89.7
Lima	WGLE(FM)†	90.7
Oxford	WMUB(FM)	88.5
Toledo	WGTE(FM)	91.3
Yellow Springs	WYSO(FM)	91.3
Youngstown	WYSU(FM)	88.5
West Union	WVXM(FM)†	89.5
Wooster	WKRW(FM)†	89.3

OKLAHOMA

Lawton	KCCU(FM)	89.3
Norman	KGOU(FM)	106.3
Oklahoma City	KROU(FM)†	105.7
Stillwater	KOSU(FM)	91.7
Tulsa	KWGS(FM)	89.5

OREGON

Ashland	KSJK(AM)	1230
	KSMF(FM)†	89.1
	KSOR(FM)	90.1
Astoria	KMUN(FM)*	91.9
Bend	KOAB(FM)†	91.3
Coos Bay	KSBA(FM)†	88.5
Eugene	KLCC(FM)	89.7
Grants Pass	KAGI(AM)†	930
Klamath Falls	KSKF(FM)†	90.9
Newport	KLCO(FM)†	90.5
Pendleton	KRBM(FM)†	90.9
Portland	KBPS(FM)	89.9
	KBPS(AM)	1450
	KOAC(AM)	550
	KOPB(FM)	91.5
Roseburg	KSRS(FM)†	91.5

PENNSYLVANIA

Erie	WQLN(FM)	91.3
Harrisburg	WITF(FM)	89.5
	WJAZ(FM)†	91.7
Mt. Pocono	WRTY(FM)†	91.1
Philadelphia	WHYY(FM)	90.9
	WRTI(FM)	90.1
Pittsburgh	WDUQ(FM)	90.5
Scranton	WVIA(FM)	89.9
State College	WPSU(FM)*	91.1

SOUTH CAROLINA

Aiken	WLJK(FM)†	89.1
Beaufort	WJWJ(FM)†	89.9
Charleston	WSCI(FM)	89.3
Columbia	WLTR(FM)	91.3
Conway	WHMC(FM)†	90.1
Greenville/Clemson	WEPR(FM)†	90.1
Rock Hill	WNSC(FM)†	88.9
Sumter	WRJA(FM)†	88.1

SOUTH DAKOTA

Brookings	KESD(FM)†	88.3
Faith	KPSD(FM)†	97.1
Lowry	KQSD(FM)†	91.9
Martin	KZSD(FM)†	102.5
Pierpont	KDSD(FM)†	90.9
Rapid City	KBHE(FM)†	89.3
Reliance	KTSD(FM)†	91.1
Sioux Falls	KRSD(FM)†	88.1
	KCSD(FM)†	90.9
Vermillion	KUSD(FM)†	89.7
	KUSD(AM)	690

TENNESSEE

Chattanooga	WUTC(FM)	88.1
Collegedale	WSMC(FM)	90.5
Jackson	WKNP(FM)†	90.1
Johnson City	WETS(FM)	89.5
Knoxville	WUOT(FM)	91.9
Memphis	WKNO(FM)	91.1
Murfreesboro	WMOT(FM)	89.5
Nashville	WPLN(FM)	90.3

TEXAS

Abilene	KACU(FM)*	89.7
Austin	KUT(FM)	90.5
Beaumont	KVLU(FM)	91.3
College Station	KAMU(FM)	90.9
Corpus Christi	KEDT(FM)	90.3
Dallas	KERA(FM)	90.1
El Paso	KTEP(FM)	88.5
Harlingen	KMBH(FM)	88.9
Houston	KUHF(FM)	88.7
	KTSU(FM)†	90.9
Lubbock	KOHM(FM)	89.1
McAllen	KHID(FM)†	88.1
Odessa	KOCV(FM)*	91.3
Redland	KLDN(FM)†	88.9
San Antonio	KSTX(FM)	89.1
Texarkana	KTXK(FM)†	91.5

UTAH

Logan	KUSU(FM)	91.5
Park City	KPCW(FM)	91.9
Salt Lake City	KUER(FM)	90.1

VERMONT

Burlington	WVPS(FM)†	107.9
Rutland	WRVT(FM)†	88.7
Windsor	WVPR(FM)	89.5

VIRGINIA

Charlottesville	WVTU(FM)†	91.9
Harrisonburg	WMRA(FM)	90.7
Lexington	WMRL(FM)†	89.9
Marion	WVTR(FM)†	91.9
Norfolk	WHRO(FM)†	90.3
	WHRV(FM)	89.5
Richmond	WCVE(FM)	88.9
Roanoke	WVTF(FM)	89.1

WASHINGTON

Bellingham	KZAZ(FM)*	91.7
Ellensburg	KNWR(FM)†	90.7
Pullman	KWSU(AM)	1250
Richland	KFAE(FM)†	89.1
Seattle	KUOW(FM)	94.9
Spokane	KPBX(FM)	91.1
Tacoma	KPLU(FM)	88.5

WEST VIRGINIA

Beckley	WVPB(FM)†	91.7
Buckhannon	WVPW(FM)†	88.9
Charleston	WVPN(FM)	88.5
Huntington	WVWV(FM)†	89.9
Martinsburg	WVEP(FM)†	88.9
Morgantown	WVPM(FM)†	90.9
Parkersburg	WVPG(FM)†	90.3
Wheeling	WVNP(FM)†	89.9

WISCONSIN

Appleton	WLFM(FM)†	91.1
Auburndale/Stevens Point	WLBL(AM)†	930
Brule	WHSA(FM)†	89.9
Delafield/Milwaukee	WHAD(FM)†	90.7
Eau Claire	WUEC(FM)†	89.7
Green Bay	WGBW(FM)†	91.5
	WPNE(FM)†	89.3
Hayward	WOJB(FM)	88.9
Highland/Dodgeville	WHHI(FM)†	91.3
Kenosha/Racine	WGTD(FM)	91.1
La Crosse	WLSU(FM)	88.9
	WHLA(FM)†	90.3
Madison	WERN(FM)	88.7
	WHA(AM)	970
Menomonie	WHWC(FM)†	88.3
	WVSS(FM)†	90.7
Milwaukee	WUWM(FM)	89.7
Park Falls	WHBM(FM)†	90.3
Rhinelander	WXPR(FM)	91.7
Wausau	WHRM(FM)†	90.9

WYOMING

Laramie	KUWR(FM)	91.9

†*Associate Station*   **Auxiliary Station*

Photo Credits

We are especially indebted to Jerome Liebling and Murray Bognovitz for their work in photographing many of the people seen on these pages and for their advice and counsel. We also want to thank National Public Radio and *Current* newspaper for making their photo files available to us. The following list includes the photographer where he or she is known.

71	Jerome Liebling
72	Steve Behrens (Ron Bornstein)
	Courtesy NPR (Tim Wirth)
73	Valerie Taylor, courtesy *Current*
75	Murray Bognovitz
77	Joyce Bland Smith, courtesy *Current* (Doug Bennet)
	Courtesy *Current* (Frank Mankiewicz)
78	Jerome Liebling
80	Lee Hansley, courtesy NPR
82	Max Hirshfeld
83	Max Hirshfeld
84	Murray Bognovitz
85	Murray Bognovitz
87	Murray Bognovitz
88	Courtesy *Current*
89	Harlee H. Little, Jr., courtesy NPR
92	Jerome Liebling
93	Courtesy NPR
94	Murray Bognovitz (Joyce Davis, Maria Hinojosa)
	Courtesy NPR (Robert Krulwich)
95	Murray Bognovitz
96	Courtesy NPR (Neal Conan, Brenda Wilson)
	Max Hirshfeld (Lynn Neary)
97	Courtesy *Current* (Robert Siegel)
	Max Hirshfeld (Linda Wertheimer)
98	Stan Barouh, courtesy *Current*
99	Harlee Little, Jr., courtesy NPR
100	Emmett Martin, courtesy *Current* (John Hockenberry)
	Staff Sgt. Michael Hughes, U.S. Army, courtesy NPR (Scott Simon)
	Courtesy NPR (Deborah Wang, John Ydstie)
	Harlee Little, Jr., courtesy NPR (Ogulnik/Wertheimer)
	Neal Conan, courtesy NPR (Deborah Amos)
	Donatella Lorch, courtesy NPR (Neal Conan)
103	Art Silverman, courtesy NPR
104	Murray Bognovitz

105	Courtesy NPR
106	Reuters/Bettmann
107	Reuters/Bettmann
110	George Lange, courtesy WHYY
112	Courtesy NPR (Georges Collinet)
	Ron Eisenberg, courtesy NPR (Miriam Makeba)
	Courtesy NPR (Annette Konan, Thomas Mapfumo)
113	Courtesy NPR (El Grande Cuba)
	Sean Barlow (Omar Peine)
114	Frank Lindner, courtesy NPR
115	Courtesy *Current*
116	Richard Howard
117	Murray Bognovitz (Peter Pennekamp)
	Don Dahler, courtesy NPR (Fiona Ritchie)
	Courtesy *Current* (Michael Feldman)
118	Courtesy *Current* (Garrison Keillor)
	Courtesy *Current* (Garrison Keillor)
	Frederic Petters, courtesy American Radio Company (Fisher/Austin)
120	Courtesy *Current* (Isabel Ilegria)
121	Paula Darte, courtesy NPR (Martin Goldsmith)
	Courtesy NPR (Leonard Slatkin, Liane Hansen)
123	Max Hirshfeld, courtesy NPR
126	Jerome Liebling
127	Courtesy Bob Edwards (Edwards and others)
	Jerome Liebling (Bob Edwards)
129	Courtesy NPR
130	Murray Bognovitz
131	Murray Bognovitz
133	Murray Bognovitz
134	Murray Bognovitz
136	Murray Bognovitz
137	Murray Bognovitz
139	Courtesy *Current*
140	Murray Bognovitz
141	Murray Bognovitz